PAUL:
man of steel and velvet

James T. Dyet

ACCENT BOOKS
Denver, Colorado

MEMBER OF
EVANGELICAL CHRISTIAN
PUBLISHERS ASSOCIATION

ACCENT BOOKS
A division of B/P Publications
12100 W. Sixth Avenue
P.O. Box 15337
Denver, Colorado 80215

Copyright © 1976 B/P Publications, Inc.
Printed in U.S.A.

Library of Congress Catalog Number: 76-9579

ISBN 0-916406-30-X

Dedication

To my parents, William and Susan Dyet, who left Scotland in 1939 but carried with them the best graces of that bonnie land.

O Scotia! my dear, my native soil!
  For whom my warmest wish to Heaven is sent!
Long may thy hardy sons of rustic toil
  Be blest with health, and peace, and sweet content!
                              —Robert Burns

Contents

Preface

He blazed a missionary trail across the Roman Empire, leaving behind him a string of young, vibrant churches. His powerful preaching persuaded a host of men and women to turn in faith to Jesus Christ for salvation. He testified before philosophers, Pharisees, rulers, rogues, soldiers, sorcerers, silversmiths, sailors and slaves. His witness for Christ even penetrated Caesar's household and claimed some of its members for the King above all kings.

It mattered not where this man preached. He was solely concerned with *whom* He preached. He preached the Lord Jesus Christ—in synagogues, on a mountain slope, in an upper chamber, in prison, by a river, in the market place, in court, aboard a ship—*everywhere!*

He was, of course, the Apostle Paul, the man God used to author thirteen New Testament epistles and to portray undying devotion to the gospel of saving grace.

This book does not trace Paul's journeys or analyze his epistles. Instead, it focuses on the man himself and highlights his dominant characteristics and convictions. As you read, keep in mind that Paul was not a super human being untouched by the temptations so common to the rank and file of Christians. He was only a human being, but he dared to follow Christ as Lord, and history shows the amazing results of that loyalty.

I hope that the pages which follow will lead you on an adventure in personal spiritual growth as you recognize that Paul's God, your heavenly Father, can enrich your life as He did Paul's—with Christlike character and unshakable convictions.

Chapter 1

The Rise and Fall of a Pharisee

The Apostle Paul, first introduced to us in the New Testament as Saul of Tarsus, was truly an extraordinary man. In a way, he led two lives. The first led up to his conversion to Christ, which must have been the last thing he expected would happen. The second led to a triumphant entrance into Heaven. What's more, he lived both lives with absolute commitment to his personal goals. He never did anything half-heartedly.

Born outside the land of the Jews, in the city of Tarsus, Saul was hardly the most likely person to become a prominent religious figure in Jerusalem. But then, as I mentioned, Saul was an extraordinary man. Not only did he become a prominent religious figure in Jerusalem, he assumed the role of champion among the Pharisees to further their cause against the Christians.

The Pharisees, you may recall, comprised an aristocratic sect in Judaism. They were extremely legalistic, proud of their religious pedigree, and jealous to maintain undisputed sway over the thinking and conduct of the Jews. Undoubtedly, their jealousy had spurred them on to plot the death of Jesus Christ. They could not stand to see Jesus' growing popularity among the Jews. Matthew describes such plotting after Jesus healed a man's paralyzed hand on the Sabbath: "Then the Pharisees went out, and held a council against him, how they might destroy him" (Matthew 12:14).

On another occasion these fanatical religionists sent an armed band to apprehend Jesus (John 7:32). But the scheme failed. The Apostle John explains: "Then came the officers to the chief priests and Pharisees; and they said unto them, Why have ye not brought him? The officers answered, Never man spoke like this man" (John 7:45, 46).

Finally, Jesus Christ was crucified, and the Pharisees thought they were rid of Him once and for all. But they were mistaken. Following the crucifixion, Jesus Christ arose and showed Himself to His disciples. Furthermore, He commissioned His disciples to carry the good news of His death and resurrection to the ends of the earth (Matthew 28:19, 20; Acts 1:8). Then He returned to Heaven (Acts 1:9). Soon His disciples had filled Jerusalem and Judea with the message of Christ.

That's when the young Pharisee, Saul, rose to prominence. But before we trace Saul's career from this point, let's get better acquainted with his background.

Saul's Early Life

Tarsus, Saul's birthplace (Acts 9:11; 21:39; 22:3), was the proud capital of the province of Cilicia. Situated 515 miles northwest of Jerusalem and 129 miles west of Antioch of Syria, Tarsus boasted a fascinating history and superb Greek culture. The Assyrians captured Tarsus around 850 B.C., and three centuries later the Persians under Cyrus claimed it.

Alexander the Great's conquests resulted in Tarsus becoming a city in the Seleucid kingdom, although it did come under the Ptolemies for awhile. During Rome's civil wars, it sided with Caesar. It must have been due to this loyalty that Augustus declared Tarsus a free city.

As a free city, Tarsus enjoyed prestige and numerous advantages. It minted its own currency, held jurisdiction over its own citizens and foreign residents, and levied taxes. In addition, Tarsus was spared the burdens of paying a land tax to Rome and housing a Roman garrison.

Education and Greek culture flourished in Tarsus. Historians point out that the city was at least equal to Athens and Alexandria in these respects. The Greek poet Aratus in the third century B.C. made Tarsus his home.

Interestingly, Paul quoted from Aratus in his address on Mars' Hill (Acts 17:28). In the second half of the first century B.C. Strabo, the Greek geographer, studied in Tarsus; and in Paul's day a number of important philosophers stretched their minds in his historic home town.

Paul grew up in a Jewish home. His family tree sprung from the best soil—the tribe of Benjamin (Philippians 3:5). This noble tribe gave Israel her first king, Saul. After King Saul's death, the Benjamites supported Saul's son Ish-bosheth. Sometime after Ish-bosheth was assassinated by the ruthless Rechab and Baanah (II Samuel 4:5-7), the tribe rallied behind David as their king. Following the death of Solomon, David's son, ten tribes of Israel split off from Judah to form a rebel nation under Jeroboam with designated cities for idolatrous worship. Only Benjamin remained with the tribe of Judah to perpetuate the worship of Jehovah in Jerusalem, God's appointed place for worship. And centuries later, when the Jews returned from exile to rebuild the walls of Jerusalem and the Temple, the tribes of Benjamin and Judah formed the foundation for the new nation.

Paul's heritage included full adherence to the Hebrew religion. He referred to himself in his preconversion years as "an Hebrew of the Hebrews" (Philippians 3:5). Although his home town was permeated with Greek culture, neither Paul nor his parents deviated from strict Hebrew beliefs and conduct. It is apparent that Paul's father was a stickler for observing the details of the Jewish law, for Paul testified before the Sanhedrin in Acts 23:6, "Men and brethren, I am a Pharisee, the son of a Pharisee."

Undoubtedly, Paul's father must have taught him the Old Testament Scriptures and instilled within him a loyalty to the Jewish law. And the teaching proved to be successful, for Paul looked back on his Jewish life and reflected that "touching the righteousness which is in the law," he was "blameless" (Philippians 3:6).

How did it come about that Paul's family settled in Tarsus? Some Biblical historians suggest that when Tarsus was part of the Seleucid kingdom one of the Seleucid kings planted a colony of Jews in Tarsus to reinforce his hold on the city. Others favor the view that Paul's family was part of the Dispersion, or Diaspora, a great company of Jews who settled throughout the Gentile nations. These Jews were uprooted either because of adverse circumstances in Palestine or because conquering rulers transported them to new locations in order to build up the population in each of their kingdoms.

The education Paul received in his early home life was nothing short of exceptional. Josephus, the famous Jewish historian, suggests that the Jews learned the law as soon as they were sensible of anything, and had it so engraven on their souls that they could recite it more easily than they could give their own names. Although this strikes us as an exaggeration, we may rest assured that at home and in a synagogue school young Paul obtained a thorough indoctrination in the details of the law, most likely in Greek. Also, since it was customary to teach every Jewish boy a trade, Paul gained skill in a trade—tent making (Acts 18:1-3).

Probably at the age of thirteen, Paul traveled to Jerusalem to pursue rabbinic training in the school of Gamaliel. We can only conjecture what profound delight this young student of the law experienced when he viewed the holy city for the first time. And, when he caught sight of the Temple—the very center of Jewish worship for centuries, his heart must have skipped a beat. Perhaps his mouth dropped open in a moment of reverential awe.

At any rate, Paul could not have chosen a better "campus" than Jerusalem or a better teacher than the famous and much revered Gamaliel (Acts 22:3).

Summa Cum Laude

Historians tell us that the usual length of study in a school like Gamaliel's was twelve years. During this period Paul's mind grasped subject matter with all the tenacity of a bulldog hanging on to a succulent bone. He memorized Scripture, the teacher's explanation of Scripture, and the immense traditional interpretations of the law of Moses. One scholar suggests that such memorization was designed to make the student's mind like a well-plastered cistern, which doesn't lose so much as a drop of the water which is poured into it.

When Paul graduated, he must have been at the head of his class, a Pharisee of the Pharisees. At least, his conduct following graduation would indicate that this was so. Consider Paul's claim in Galatians 1:13a,14: "For ye have heard of my conversation [conduct] in time past in the Jews' religion, how ... I ... profited in the Jews' religion above many my equals in mine own nation, being more exceedingly zealous of the traditions of my fathers."

Come of Age

Paul and Jesus Christ were contemporaries. Yet, there is no reason to suppose that Paul met Jesus during His earthly ministry. None of Paul's epistles makes even the slightest reference to such a meeting. It would appear that Paul returned to Tarsus when he completed his rabbinic studies. The Biblical account focuses on the emergence of Paul in Jerusalem sometime after our Lord's ascension into Heaven.

Eventually this zealous Pharisee became a member of the Sanhedrin in Jerusalem; at least this seems apparent from Paul's statement in Acts 26:10 that he cast his vote with the Sanhedrin to destroy Christians. As a member of this Jewish council, Paul enjoyed both fame and influence, for the Sanhedrin functioned as the highest politico-religious body of that period of Jewish history. Comprised of priests, elders and scribes, the

70-member Sanhedrin exercised uncontested rule over the civil and religious life of the nation.

We meet Paul for the first time in Scripture at the martyrdom of Stephen, the faithful deacon who preached Christ to the Sanhedrin (Acts 7).

Do you remember what took place on that day of infamy? The members of the Sanhedrin could not stomach Stephen's witness. And when he accused them of betraying and murdering the Messiah, they flew into a wild rage. They gnashed their teeth, while Stephen gazed into Heaven and declared that He saw Jesus there at God's right hand. Then they rushed him, dragged him outside the city, laid down their garments at Saul's feet, and bashed in Stephen's body with stones until he drew his last breath.

This is how Saul got his first taste of Christian blood. It was not enough; he was thirsty for more.

White-Hot Hatred

Stephen's murder marked the beginning of a reign of terror for the church. Acts 8:1 states: "And at that time there was a great persecution against the church which was at Jerusalem; and they were all scattered abroad throughout the regions of Judaea and Samaria, except the apostles."

Those were horrendous days for the followers of Jesus Christ. The fires of persecution were raging, first in Jerusalem, next in Judea, then in Samaria. The religious rulers of the Jews were determined to exterminate all who believed in and preached the risen Christ of Calvary. And guess who led the assault. That's right, bloodthirsty Saul of Tarsus. "As for Saul, he made havock of the church, entering into every house, and haling men and women committed them to prison" (Acts 8:3).

Just how vicious were Saul's attacks against the church? Later in his life, Paul recalled: "Many of the saints did I shut up in prison, having received authority from the chief priests; and when they were put to death, I gave my voice against them. And I punished them oft in every synagogue, and compelled them to blaspheme; and being exceedingly mad against them, I persecuted them even unto strange [foreign] cities" (Acts 26:10,11).

Now, here's an amazing fact. Persecution builds strong Christians. It puts iron in our muscles and starch in our spine, so that we stand firm for the cause of Christ. Saul's relentless, hateful attacks against the first-century Christians failed to silence their witness. In fact, the result was the very opposite. The Scripture declares triumphantly, "Therefore they that were scattered abroad went every where preaching the word" (Acts 8:4). Likely, some went as far as Damascus in Syria.

So Saul planned a trip to Damascus.

Journey to a New Life

Before departing for Damascus, Saul went

to the president of the Sanhedrin, the high priest, to request authorization to arrest and bring back Christians from Damascus. It mattered not whether women were among the prey; Saul was quite willing to slap chains on them, too, and drag them back to the capital (Acts 9:1,2).

With legal documents in hand Saul traveled toward Damascus with an armed entourage. The heat of the eastern sun was no more intense than the scorching hatred Saul harbored for the believers he could hardly wait to get his hands on. We may well suppose that he allowed no one in his company to proceed at less than a brisk pace. The horses must have built up a heavy sweat on their hides and froth on the bits as they galloped along. Saul was getting closer and closer to his quarry. He was getting closer, too, to one of the most dramatic events in history—his conversion to Jesus Christ.

Near the outskirts of Damascus a dazzling light from Heaven struck Saul's troop. Its glare, which was as brilliant as the midday sun, forced Saul and his men to fall to the ground (Acts 9:3,4; 26:13,14a). Then a voice, intelligible only to Saul, thundered its way into the depths of Saul's troubled soul.

"Saul, Saul, why persecutest thou me?" the voice demanded (Acts 9:4b).

When Saul inquired, "Who art thou, Lord?" the voice replied, "I am Jesus whom thou persecutest: it is hard for thee to kick against the pricks" (verse 5).

Jesus' reply and subsequent question spill

over with significance. His reply makes it plain that He identifies with us in our afflictions. Nothing escapes His attention. When a persecutor raises a hand against us he is, in fact, raising a hand against our Saviour and Lord. His question makes it plain that Saul had been under smarting conviction. The vicious persecution he had been directing sprang from a troubled conscience. In his frustration, Saul had been lashing out violently against the church. Undoubtedly, Stephen's message and victorious death had struck like a dagger into Saul's soul.

Our Lord's indictment drained all the religious pride from the young Pharisee. Saul trembled before the righteous Judge, the risen Christ. Blinded by the brilliant light, but no longer blind to the truth concerning the Saviour, Saul cast himself upon His grace and mercy (verse 6).

The Pharisee had fallen. Saul lay on the Damascus Road as an empty vessel. But the Lord was about to raise him and give him abundant, eternal life. Soon He would fill him with divine love and power, so necessary for the fulfillment of the amazing plan He had for him.

Chapter 2

The Making
of an Apostle

According to a certain story, a spiteful, malicious old Scotsman by the name of Kline came to Christ, strangely enough, through his misunderstanding of a line of a familiar hymn. One day while lying in wait behind a roadside clump of bushes and expecting to ambush a victim of his hate, Kline observed a group of children approaching on the road. They were singing, and as they drew nearer the old villain thought he heard them sing, "Jesus died for auld man Kline, and Jesus died for me." Not realizing that they were actually singing, "Jesus died for all mankind . . ." the rogue was deeply touched and in tears confessed his sin and asked Jesus to save him. That roadside occurrence led to the transformation of the man's life.

It was also a roadside occurrence that changed Paul's life, wasn't it? On the road to Damascus he met the Lord of glory, and nothing was the same again. Looking back to that remarkable occasion, Paul declared that he had been apprehended by Christ Jesus (Philippians 3:12). In other words, according to Paul, Jesus Christ got a grip on him and wouldn't let go.

Doesn't this do something for you? Doesn't it get things stirring down deep in your soul to know that Jesus Christ's power is so great? Just think of it, becoming a follower of Jesus Christ was the farthest thing from Paul's thinking when he traveled the Damascus Road. His whole attention focused on destroying all who trusted in the Saviour in Damascus. He was obsessed with his scheme to sweep Christianity off the earth once and for all. He never dreamed that he would become a believer himself. But, then, he had not reckoned on the power of Jesus Christ. Knowing that Jesus Christ turned Paul's life inside out and right side up ought to encourage us to keep on praying for and witnessing to those friends and relatives who we were beginning to feel were beyond hope.

Of course the living Saviour laid hold on Paul not only to save him but also to save multitudes of Gentiles through the ministry which Paul would have in the Gentile world. In no uncertain terms Jesus Christ informed Paul, "I have appeared unto thee for this purpose, to make thee a minister and a witness both of these things which thou hast seen, and of those things in which I will appear unto thee; Delivering thee from the people, and from the Gentiles, unto whom now I send thee" (Acts 26:16b,17).

The big question is, how did our Lord make Paul a suitable messenger to the Gentiles? If we can discover the answer, we ought to be able to gain some important tips on how we, too, can serve God successfully on behalf of a generation which so desperately needs to get personally acquainted with Jesus Christ.

His to Command

Right from the start of his new life in Christ Paul showed an unhesitating obedience to the Master. "Arise, and go into the city, and it shall be told thee what thou must do" (Acts 9:6b). This order from the Master to Paul on the Damascus Road may appear to us to be hardly worth the space it occupies in the Bible until we put ourselves in Paul's sandals. Then the order looms mighty big. We begin to think about the fact that the dazzling light from Heaven had blinded Paul—at least temporarily. And we remind ourselves that Paul would be helpless in Damascus in such a condition. Not knowing whether the Christians in the city would take advantage of his handicap as an opportunity to kill him, Paul could have protested, "Lord, please don't tell me to go into Damascus. How about picking a different city—a nice, quiet, neutral city?" But he didn't. "And Saul arose from the earth; . . . they led him by the hand, and brought him into Damascus" (Acts 9:8).

Praying Earnestly

An appointed and prepared believer in Damascus by the name of Ananias was instructed by the Lord to proceed to the home of Judas on Straight Street and ask to see Paul. Paul would be expecting the visit, for the Lord had revealed to him in a vision how Ananias would come and put his hands on him "that he might receive his sight" (verse 12). Interestingly, while giving directions to Ananias, the Lord commented concerning Paul: "Behold, he prayeth" (verse 11).

This in itself suggests that Paul had become a new man—a new creation in Christ (II Corinthians 5:17). Just as a newborn baby's crying proves that life is present, even so Paul's prayers throughout the three days of his blindness (Acts 9:9) proved that he had been born into God's family. The Holy Spirit had taken up residence in Paul's heart and was prompting him to cry, "Abba, Father" (Galatians 4:6).

Undoubtedly Paul had *said* numerous prayers in his preconversion years, for Pharisees were noted for saying prayers. Jesus must have been referring to the Pharisees when He warned, "And when thou prayest, thou shalt not be as the hypocrites are: for they love to pray standing in the synagogues and in the corners of the streets, that they may be seen of men" (Matthew 6:5). And you may recall the story Jesus told about a Pharisee who prayed *with himself* in the Temple. His prayers bounced back off the ceiling, for his heart wasn't right with God (Luke 18:10-14). So we may assume that Paul had said prayers before he believed on Christ, but this episode in Damascus marked the first time Paul had really prayed.

Was he praying for God to restore his sight? Not likely, for Acts 9:12 suggests that the Lord had assured Paul that his sight would return at the time of Ananias' visit to him. In all probability Paul was immersed in intense confession of his crimes against the Lord's people. And, of course, in the process he was getting better acquainted with the One whose grace plunges even the vilest sins into the depths of the sea of His forgetfulness.

In a way, the Lord used temporary blindness to shut out the world from Paul's thinking so that his full attention would focus on spiritual concerns. When sight returned to Paul, his vision was filled with Jesus Christ and the harvest fields waiting to be reaped.

Learning What to Preach

Someone forged this solid advice for preachers: Don't preach because you have to say something; preach because you have something to say! Paul's preaching left no doubt in the minds of his listeners that he had something to say. And he knew that he had something to say. "Woe is unto me, if I preach not the gospel!" Paul volunteered in I Corinthians 9:16.

What was this all-important message (the

gospel) Paul preached so urgently? How did he acquire it? Let's let Paul himself answer both of these questions.

He begins the fifteenth chapter of I Corinthians by writing, "I declare unto you the gospel which I preached unto you." Then he presents a clear definition of the gospel, which emphasizes four essentials: 1) "Christ died for our sins according to the scriptures"; 2) "he was buried"; 3) "he rose again the third day according to the scriptures"; and 4) "he was seen."

You can understand why the word "gospel" identifies Paul's message—and ours, for it means "good news" in the language of the New Testament. The four essentials Paul stressed in his definition combine to form *good news*, actually, the greatest news of all time. It is personal: Christ died for our sins. It is triumphant: Christ was buried, but He arose from the grave. It is factual: Christ, the risen Saviour, was seen by a great host of eye-witnesses.

Is it any wonder Paul testified in Romans 1:16, "For I am not ashamed of the gospel of Christ: for it is the power of God unto salvation to every one that believeth"? How can anyone who knows the saving power of the living Christ be ashamed to pass the good news along to others?

Suppose a doctor in charge of the hospital care of cancer patients received the wonderful news that a cure for cancer had been found. Would he be ashamed to share that news with his patients? Of course not. He would hurry to pass along the news, and his joy in doing so would be tremendous. Why, then, shouldn't we pass along the gospel enthusiastically and joyfully? Paul is our example in this.

Now let's turn our attention to Paul's answer to the second question: How did he acquire a knowledge of the gospel message? The first chapter of Galatians contains Paul's explanation, which deserves our closest attention.

Before we get the full answer, we learn first how Paul did *not* gain his knowledge of the gospel. "I neither received it of man, neither was I taught it," he affirms in verse 12a. In verse 17 he volunteers, "Neither went I up to Jerusalem to them which were apostles before me." These affirmations rule out any possibility that Paul's gospel message was a human concoction.

Here's how Paul learned about the gospel of grace, "by the revelation of Jesus Christ" (Galatians 1:12). Following the Damascus Road conversion, God enrolled Paul in a "private seminary"—very private, for Paul was the only student. The campus for the instruction was Arabia, according to verse 17. There in the deserts of Arabia, perhaps not too far from Damascus, the triune God opened Paul's heart and mind to understand the doctrines of grace. For three years Paul meditated on the Old Testament Scriptures, communed with the Lord, and fixed his desires on serving Christ (verse 18). Then he was ready to proclaim the gospel to the world.

In Arabia Paul left the burden of Pharisaic

lawkeeping in the sands and emerged with the gospel of grace in his heart.

What God did in Paul's experience was certainly unique, but there is a sense in which Paul's experience must be shared by all who would be His spokesmen. There simply is no substitute for private communion with God before commencing a public career for God. Moses, David, Elijah, and John the Baptist, like Paul, had their wilderness "quiet time" before God launched them into active service. And let's not forget that Pentecost was preceded by a lengthy prayer meeting. The apostles were shut in to pray before they were sent out with power to preach.

Many Christians are turning to personal Bible study and prayer today. The increased interest in meditating upon God and His Word is gratifying to observe, particularly among our Christian youth. It is not too much to expect that a great spiritual harvest will result from this spiritual enterprise. Psalm 1:3 promises that whoever delights in God's Word and meditates faithfully in it "shall be like a tree planted by the rivers of water, that bringeth forth his fruit in his season; his leaf also shall not wither; and whatsoever he doeth shall prosper."

Interestingly, when Paul concluded his "seminary" training in Arabia, his first preaching station was Damascus (Galatians 1:17). Those he had intended to persecute three years earlier enjoyed the privilege of hearing him preach the message God had burned into his inner man.

And where do you suppose God's specially prepared apostle preached next? At home. That's right. Paul went to Syria and Cilicia (verse 21), which included his home town, Tarsus. Thus, he proved that God had performed a genuine work of transforming grace in his life, for he gave those who knew him best the opportunity to scrutinize his life and message.

Paul's apostolic career had begun. God had made an apostle out of a former Pharisee. Eventually, the whole world would know that God's work was magnificent and lasting.

Chapter 3

Christ Is Lord

I have heard more than a few well-intentioned speakers advise their hearers, "Make Christ Lord in your life." I hope they really meant to say, "Submit to Christ's Lordship." You see, no one can *make* Jesus Christ Lord; He is Lord already.

The Apostle Paul testified that "Jesus Christ is Lord" (Philippians 2:11).

Undoubtedly, it was largely due to Paul's firm conviction that Jesus Christ is Lord that he served Him with unwavering devotion. Paul's first response to Jesus Christ included a reference to His Lordship: "What shall I do, Lord?" (Acts 22:10a). And his final benediction in Scripture contains a similar reference: "The Lord Jesus Christ be with thy spirit" (II Timothy 4:22). From the beginning of his Christian pilgrimage to its victorious consummation the Apostle Paul knew that Jesus Christ is Lord. And he submitted to this Lordship without the slightest hesitation.

Kurios is the New Testament word for Lord. Greek slaves employed *kurios* as a title of respect for their owner or master. It became the title of the Roman Emperors in the Greek-speaking world. To the Greeks, the Emperor was *kurios*, whereas to the Latin-speaking population he was *dominus* (the Latin word for lord). *Kurios* was also applied to the pagan deities. Every god received from the Greeks the prefix *kurios* attached to its name. Finally, the Greeks used *kurios* to translate the Hebrew word *Jehovah* from the Hebrew Scriptures into the Greek version.

You can see, then, that when Paul and the other New Testament writers call Jesus *kurios* (Lord), they are presenting Him to us as our Owner-Master, the King of all kings (the supreme Emperor), and Deity. With each of these meanings in mind, let's roam Paul's writings to learn what all of this meant to him—and what it ought to mean to us.

Master-Owner

Paul urged people to believe on Jesus Christ, not simply as the One who died to redeem them, but also as the One who lives to rule them. "Believe on the Lord Jesus Christ, and thou shalt be saved," he informed the Philippian jailer (Acts 16:31). "If thou shalt confess with thy mouth the Lord Jesus, and shalt believe in thine heart that God hath raised him from the dead, thou shalt be saved," he announces in Romans 10:9. And to the Colossian church he charged, "As ye have therefore received Christ Jesus the Lord, so walk ye in him" (Colossians 2:6).

Notice how the Lordship of Christ, central to each of the preceding verses, relates to the initial act of salvation. We may seriously question whether anyone can receive eternal life who does not recognize that Jesus Christ possesses the sovereign right to be his Lord. The fact is, the blood Jesus shed to cleanse each of us was sufficient also to claim each of us. This is why Paul explains in I Corinthians 6:19b,20: "Ye are not your own. For ye are bought with a price: therefore glorify God in your body, and in your spirit, which are God's."

This matter of being purchased with the blood of the Lord Jesus Christ relates to the Biblical doctrine of redemption. Paul writes in Romans 3:24,25a: "Being justified freely by his grace through the redemption that is in Christ Jesus: Whom God hath set forth to be a propitiation through faith in his blood." God's Son redeemed us Christians by His blood.

There are three forms of the word, "redeem," in the New Testament. The first implies to buy in a market. The second means to buy out of the market and remove from further sale. And the third signifies to loose or set free. Each meaning gives us a better understanding of our redemption. Jesus Christ bought us in sin's slave market. Paul states: "Ye were the servants [slaves] of sin"

(Romans 6:17). Furthermore, He bought us out of sin's slave market and removed us from further sale; we will never belong to sin again. Finally, He set us free—free to serve God and righteousness (Romans 6:18,22).

Paul never lost sight of the fact that the Lord had purchased him with His blood, released him from sin's bondage, and given him the freedom to follow Him as a devoted apostle. How often in his letters Paul refers to himself as "a servant of Jesus Christ"! (See, for example, Romans 1:1; Philippians 1:1; Titus 1:1.)

Again, the New Testament setting improves our understanding of a word; in this case, "servant." The word is *doulos*, and signifies "bondslave." A bondslave differed from other slaves, or servants, for he was born into slavery and would remain a slave until death. Throughout his entire life he belonged to another. All his desires would focus on doing his master's will. All his energies and abilities would be devoted to his master's use.

Can you get the impact of Paul's words? He gladly owns Jesus Christ, the Lord, as His Master-Owner. He became the Lord's slave by being born again. He would spend the rest of his life as the Lord's slave. He would employ all his energies and abilities to do the will of his Lord.

Not long ago the world was introduced to a Japanese soldier, who had been hiding in the jungles of the Philippines for over thirty years. As far as he was concerned, the Second World War had not ended. He was determined to resist the enemy until orders came from his superiors to cease. Only a summons from his commander-in-chief convinced him that he could put World War II behind him and enter civilian life. His willingness to obey orders under far from favorable circumstances resembles Paul's faithfulness to the Lord Jesus Christ.

What might happen in our communities if a majority of Christians were as dedicated to Jesus Christ, recognizing that He is indeed our Master-Owner? Excuses for not serving Him would vanish as quickly as soap bubbles landing on cactus. Missionary candidates would receive their necessary support in record time. Church services would be crowded. The unsaved would receive a clear witness. Needy persons would get compassionate help. Businesses would be transformed. So many good things would result.

The Lordship of Christ does indeed beckon us to submit to His ownership, to yield all that we are and have to His sovereign control.

King of All Kings

Paul further believed that Jesus Christ will eventually set up His kingdom on the earth. He will descend from Heaven with His raptured saints to seize control of our troubled planet, demonstrating His absolute right to be Lord over all the earth.

Here are a few passages from Paul's letters which broadcast in advance the thrilling news of Christ's reign. As you read these, stretch your hope to that future glorious reign, and sample some of its delights right now.

"The God of our Lord Jesus Christ . . . raised him from the dead, and set him at his own right hand in the heavenly places, Far above all principality, and power, and might, and dominion, and every name that is named, not only in this world [age], but also in that which is to come: And hath put all things under his feet" (Ephesians 1:17a,20b-22a).

"Wherefore God also hath highly exalted him, and given him a name which is above every name: That at the name of Jesus every knee should bow . . . And that every tongue should confess that Jesus Christ is Lord, to the glory of God the Father" (Philippians 2:9-11).

"Who hath delivered us from the power of darkness, and hath translated us into the kingdom of his dear Son . . . Christ in you, the hope of glory" (Colossians 1:13,27).

Perhaps all of this explains why Paul did not crusade to overthrow the Roman government. He understood that it was a part of the evil world system over which Satan holds dominion, but he understood, too, that God maintains a perfect schedule. In His good time God will dispatch His Son from Heaven to seize control of our rebellious planet. Jesus will return to the earth with His raptured saints and inaugurate His perfect kingdom.

On the other hand, Paul didn't stick his head in the sand, hoping to ignore the march of wickedness. Nor did he fret and stew over gloomy world conditions. On the contrary, the apostle to the Gentiles conducted himself as an ideal citizen and endeavored to exert a positive influence on society.

Like Paul, we don't expect world conditions to improve before the Lord comes with His saints to set up His kingdom. Why should we? The Bible shows that the state of things will be dreadful—at their worst—just prior to Christ's return. Shakespeare had one of his characters in *Hamlet* suggest, "There's something rotten in the state of Denmark." When human history runs its full course there will be something rotten in every "state." But we should follow Paul's example and strive to be ideal citizens until we meet our Sovereign face to face.

Paul's writings contain plenty of challenging instructions for fulfilling our duty to government. As Christians, God holds us responsible to pray for local and national leaders, pay taxes, obey the laws of the land, honor our leaders, and as much as possible lead a peaceable life (I Timothy 2:1-3; Romans 12:18; 13:1-7; Titus 3:1,2). Anything less than this constitutes a gross dereliction of Christian duty.

Obviously Paul's convictions in this regard concur with our Lord's teaching that His people are "the salt of the earth" (Matthew 5:13). Just as salt has a preserving effect on what it pervades, even so we who belong to the King of kings ought to preserve society from rapid moral decay and rottenness.

The challenge of this came home to me vividly when my wife and I attended a precinct caucus prior to the 1976 national elections. The caucus, held in a neighbor's home, proved to be extremely interesting. About 35 residents in our precinct crowded into the family room, discussed political and moral issues, declared their views on these, and elected five delegates to carry their feelings to the county convention and support candidates (including a presidential candidate) who would represent them well in government.

But there is another reason why the caucus proved to be interesting. The group elected me with the greatest number of votes to be one of their delegates. Apparently, my expressed views made sense to them.

Now, here's the challenge I carried away from that caucus meeting: what far-reaching influence might Christians exert by involving themselves in public affairs. Since only a minority of citizens take an active part in politics beyond voting at the polls, why shouldn't Christians comprise a sizable segment of this minority? We could rally support for candidates who stand for high principles and are willing to resist godless influences. As I see it, such positive involvement would add just the right pinch of "salt" to a critical part of our modern culture.

Remember what Paul advised the Christians at Philippi? "Be blameless and harmless, the sons of God, without rebuke, in the midst of a crooked and perverse nation, among whom ye shine as lights in the world" (Philippians 2:15). The opportunity to be the King's representatives awaits only our personal dedication and ambition.

Exalted Son of God

As we have already learned, *kurios* (lord) is the Greek translation of the Hebrew word for *Jehovah*. Its application to the name of Jesus Christ signifies that He is God. Indeed He is, the exalted Son of God.

Paul was firmly persuaded that Jesus Christ is the risen Son of God. He advised the church at Rome that the gospel concerned God's "Son Jesus Christ our Lord, which was made of the seed of David according to the flesh; And declared to be the Son of God with power, according to the spirit of holiness, by the resurrection from the dead" (Romans 1:3,4).

To the Philippian believers Paul emphasized that Jesus Christ "being in the form of God, thought it not robbery to be equal with God" (Philippians 2:6). By this, Paul was expressing the great truth that Jesus Christ shares eternally the same essential nature and rank as the Father.

What an indictment Paul's inspired writings deliver against so many today who deny Jesus Christ's deity! It is not sufficient to believe that our Lord was simply a good man, whose extraordinary life began in a stable at Bethlehem and terminated on a cross outside Jerusalem. Nor is it enough to believe that He was the greatest prophet who ever lived and preached. Such a person could not link lost mankind and a holy God together. Only a perfect representative of God and man could do this. Only the God-Man—the Lord Jesus Christ—could satisfy the righteous demands of God and serve as a suitable Substitute for sinners. Jesus affirmed, "I am the way, the truth, and the life: no man cometh unto the Father, but by me" (John 14:6). And Paul testified to this truth in I Timothy 2:5: "For there is one God, and one mediator between God and men, the man Christ Jesus."

Several decades ago, when liberalism was invading Protestant seminaries and teaching among other things that Jesus was only a man, a godly seminary professor engaged his theology students in a valuable exercise. "Gentlemen," he announced, "your assignment is to study how the New Testament pictures Jesus Christ. Divide sheets of paper into three columns. In the first column list all the New Testament references which describe Jesus Christ as God. Use the second column to list the New Testament references which describe Him as the God-Man. Reserve the third column for the New Testament references which describe Him as only a man."

When the students had finished the assignment, the professor called for the results. The first and second columns bulged with New Testament references proclaiming Jesus Christ as perfect God and perfect man. The third column, which was supposed to contain references describing Him as only a man, contained not a single reference. Thus, the witness of Scripture to the divine nature of Jesus Christ made an indelible mark on a group of future ministers of the *Lord* Jesus Christ.

Paul's conviction that Jesus is Lord—Master, Sovereign, and Deity—acted as a driving force in his life, propelling him ever forward to make Christ known. He never relaxed his zeal for Christ, because he never compromised his conviction that he was serving the Lord. No work on earth could compare in importance with that of presenting the Lord of glory to others.

We, too, belong to the Lord, if we have trusted in Him. He is our Master, Sovereign, and divine Redeemer. We have no greater privilege than to serve Him as Lord.

During the years when China was open to missionary activity, an outstanding young missionary established unusually effective rapport with the Chinese. It was clear that his life and ministry were making an impact for Jesus Christ. Reports of his winning ways among the Chinese reached a British oil firm that needed a public relations figure who could persuade the Chinese to cooperate with the company's drilling efforts.

The need for such a person was crucial. So crucial, in fact, that the oil company offered the missionary a fabulous salary if he would join their organization. He refused, but the oil firm tried again. They raised the salary offer. But still the missionary turned down the opportunity.

Finally, the British oil executives pleaded with the missionary to join their company. "Name your salary requirement. Regardless of how steep you make it, we are prepared to meet it," they explained.

"Why, you have it all wrong," countered the missionary; "even the first salary offer you made was more than adequate. It's just this—the job isn't important enough!"

Nothing is as important as serving the Lord. Paul advises, "Therefore, my beloved brethren, be ye stedfast, unmoveable, always abounding in the work of the Lord, forasmuch as ye know that your labour is not in vain in the Lord" (I Corinthians 15:58).

Chapter 4

That Rare Quality—Humility

Any Christian who sings his own praises in this life may end up as an ill-at-ease soloist at the judgment seat of Christ.

The goal of Christian living is to direct honor and praise to the Lord. Paul blazed the trail for us in this, for his watchword was: "He that glorieth, let him glory in the Lord" (II Corinthians 10:17).

There's no doubt about it, Paul possessed that rare quality—humility. It characterized his preaching, his writing, and his life style.

Case in point: At Lystra Paul perceived that a lame man had faith to be healed. He commanded him to stand up. Instantly the man leaped to his feet and walked (Acts 14:8-10). The miracle had a profound effect on the spectators. They clamored to worship Paul and his coworker Barnabas. They were absolutely convinced that these two strangers were Jupiter and Mercurius, chief gods. "The gods are come down to us," they shouted. Then they brought oxen and flowers to the city gates for a public ceremony of sacrificing and praising.

Lesser men than the Apostle Paul might have looked upon the crowd's reaction as the best thing that ever happened to them and considered it an opportunity to command the crowd to pay them homage and serve their interests. But Paul displayed proper humility; and so did Barnabas. They "ran in among the people, crying out, And saying, Sirs, why do ye these things? We also are men of like passions with you, and preach unto you that ye should turn from these vanities unto the living God" (verses 14,15a).

It wasn't natural for Paul to be humble; it was supernatural—God had done a work of grace in his life. Remember that Paul had been a Pharisee prior to his conversion to Christ. The Pharisees, you will recall, were noted for their extreme pride. Jesus accused them of sounding a trumpet before them in the synagogues and in the streets that they might have the glory of men, and praying conspicuously in the synagogues and in the streets to be seen of men (Matthew 6:2,4).

The Jewish Talmud lists several classifications of Pharisees, two of which are particularly illustrative of the false humility and real pride of Paul's former religious associates. They are *The Tumbling Pharisees* and *The Bleeding Pharisees.* A tumbling Pharisee always had his head hanging down in order to appear humble. A bleeding Pharisee tried his best to get others to admire him. His trick was to close his eyes, or cover them with his hands, as he walked along, so that he could not look upon a woman. Unable to see where he was going, he would crash into buildings and emerge bruised and bleeding. Thus, he earned the name, *The Bleeding Pharisee.*

But God took Paul out of Pharisaism when He saved him. And He also took Pharisaism out of Paul. Result—Paul emerged as a Christian with a humble attitude toward salvation, spirituality and service.

Saved by Grace

Don't be surprised to learn that many religious persons just won't buy Paul's teaching about salvation. As a matter of fact, some of them would just as soon cut what he wrote about the way to eternal life right out of the Bible. The crux of the controversy is this, Paul taught that everyone—even a religious person—is a sinner, totally incapable of earning his way into Heaven. That's mighty tough on those who point to their growing pile of good works and say, "Please, God, I'd rather do it myself." Of course they will end up as the losers, for what Paul wrote in the Bible was inspired by God Himself (II Timothy 3:16). Those who oppose Paul's teaching oppose God. And God has never lost a battle!

For sure, pride gets battered by Paul's teaching about salvation. A religious do-gooder who reads Paul's epistles soon learns that the apostle didn't pull any punches. For example, in his letter to the Ephesians and in his letter to Titus Paul hit hard at the notion that a man can work his way into Heaven. He wrote in Ephesians 2:8,9, "For by grace are ye saved through faith; and that not of yourselves; it is the gift of God: Not of works, lest any man should boast." And he instruct-ed Titus that salvation is "not by works of righteousness which we have done" (Titus 3:5).

Paul viewed human nature as corrupt. Even a cursory reading of Romans 3 uncovers this fact. As a result of his helpless condition, sinful man has no recourse but to swallow his pride, admit that he is just what God says he is—a Hell-deserving sinner (Romans 3:23; 6:23), and avail himself of God's grace by trusting in Jesus Christ as Lord and Saviour (Romans 10:9,10).

Of course, Paul didn't prescribe medicine, which he hadn't taken. Even after he had repented and put his trust in Christ, he called himself, "chief" of sinners (I Timothy 1:15).

Spiritual Attainment: No Room for Pride

Lighthouses don't blow horns; they just shine. This is how it ought to be in the Christian life. Rather than tooting our own horn, we Christians should simply let our light shine. This would be best, for Jesus com-manded, "Let your light so shine before men, that they may see your good works, and glorify your Father which is in heaven" (Matthew 5:16). The Apostle Paul urged the Christians at Philippi to be lights, shining in the midst of a crooked and perverse generation (Philippians 2:15). So it seems quite clear that God wants us to lead exemplary lives without the "Jack Horner" effect; that is, without boasting, "What a good Christian am I."

Paul never boasted about his spiritual attainment. Although he was an outstanding Christian, he gave due credit to the mighty working of divine grace in his life. He admitted, "By the grace of God I am what I am" (I Corinthians 15:10a).

You have heard some persons brag about how high up "Sunshine Mountain" they have climbed, haven't you? They make it a must to tell you how they spend hours at a time in personal devotions, gaining *new messages* from the Lord. They inform you that they are "totally dedicated" to the Lord. They say, "I just wish other Christians were living the crucified life I enjoy." They never seem to take into account the fact that pride is a sin—even when it is couched in spiritual-sounding language.

Interestingly, when Paul described an outstanding spiritual experience he had, he used guarded language. He preferred to keep the lid closed on what the experience was like, and focused on the practical lessons we can all learn from it. Second Corinthians 12 carries the story.

Paul had received a vision about 14 years

before he penned Second Corinthians. He got a glimpse of Paradise and heard things which he was not at liberty to divulge. In order to protect Paul from getting an overinflated ego about this unique experience, God permitted some kind of affliction ("thorn in the flesh" —verse 7) to buffet Paul. Paul prayed three times for God to remove the affliction, but God refused to do so. Instead, He supplied Paul with enough grace to endure it. Thus, the abiding affliction jabbed Paul's memory about how necessary it was to depend upon God for strength and help at all times. Paul learned through this to say, "Most gladly therefore will I rather glory in my infirmities, that the power of Christ may rest upon me . . . when I am weak, then am I strong" (II Corinthians 12:9,10).

Let's not conclude from this passage of Scripture that it is wrong for us Christians to share with one another what God has been doing in our lives. It is good for the redeemed of the Lord to edify one another in this way. But we should avoid like the plague the tendency to engage in one-upmanship. A testimony time should never degenerate into a "Can-you-top- this?" episode.   With due humility we ought to magnify God, whose grace has extended to us undeserving, inadequate and slow-to-improve servants of the King.

God's Humble Servant

For those who expect ministers of the

gospel and their churches to show humility in all things the religious section of the newspaper can be shocking. *We are the biggest, the fastest-growing,* and *the best*—these claims cover the pages like gaudy billboards along the highways that advertise: "Best meals east of the Mississippi," "Biggest pizzas this side of Italy," "Finest motel in town."

Granted, churches need to promote their services in order to persuade the complacent to attend, but boasting, about ourselves is always out of place—even in the media.

Where in Scripture did Paul boast about how great he was? When did he compare himself with the other apostles as being the best of the bunch? Quite to the contrary Paul affirmed: "We dare not make ourselves of the number, or compare ourselves with some that commend themselves: but they measuring themselves by themselves, and comparing themselves among themselves, are not wise" (II Corinthians 10:12).

Although Paul must have been the most widely used preacher in the first century, he never got things out of focus. He was confident that he could do all things through Christ (Philippians 4:13). And he was equally confident that apart from this divine enablement he could do nothing. He explained to the Corinthians: "Not that we are sufficient of ourselves to think any thing as of ourselves; but our sufficiency is of God" (II Corinthians 3:5).

Christian work does carry its share of

temptations to those who engage in it. Preachers can succumb to the temptation to be proud of their sermon delivery, their new edifices, the economic status of their members, the number of converts they have won, growing attendance, trained choirs, ad infinitum. Christian musicians and soloists can fall victim to the applause and adulation of their audiences. There is always the need for every Christian worker, therefore, to consider himself as only the far-from-adequate instrument which is available to God to use when, where and how He chooses.

About a century ago the great Baptist preacher, Charles Haddon Spurgeon, offered an interesting observation along this line. He commented: "We have plenty of people nowadays who could not kill a mouse without publishing it in the *Gospel Gazette*. Samson killed a lion and said nothing about it; the Holy Spirit finds modesty so rare that He takes care to record it. Say much of what the Lord has done for you, but say little of what you have done for the Lord. Do not utter a self-glorifying sentence!"

It is this kind of attitude Paul expressed in II Corinthians 4:5: "For we preach not ourselves, but Christ Jesus the Lord; and ourselves your servants for Jesus' sake." It is this attitude which honors Jesus Christ, for He Himself displayed it most consistently. His earthly life was occupied with a ministry to others, and on the cross He gave Himself for us.

Humility does seem to be a rare quality in

this braggadocio era, but there is hope that we shall see more of it as the church returns to a more familiar acquaintance with Paul's view of the servant's relationship to his Master.

Chapter 5

Fully Persuaded

Credibility gap. It's an ugly term, isn't it? We use it to refer to the distance which lies between elected officials and the voters' readiness to believe what these officials tell them.

It is hard to say just when "credibility gap" slipped into our vocabulary. Perhaps it made its debut during the Francis Gary Powers incident. In 1960 Powers was flying a U-2 high over Russia when sophisticated Russian weaponry brought him down. The Russians insisted that the U-2 was on a spy mission, taking surveillance photos. At first the United States Government denied the Russians' charges, claiming that Powers had merely strayed off-course. Later, however, the U.S. owned up to the fact that for three years prior to the Powers' episode the Russian countryside had been unwittingly smiling into U-2 candid cameras. Americans were appalled to think that their leaders had forged a lie. The credibility gap had emerged.

Today the credibility gap resembles the Grand Canyon. Watergate, unfulfilled promises, and sex scandals, like giant wedges, have come between politicians and people with the result that people are asking, "Who can you believe anymore?"

Good question. Fortunately, there is an answer. You can believe God.

Paul Believed God

A most spectacular thing happened to Paul when he was on the high seas. He was a prisoner at the time, headed for Rome to stand trial for alleged crimes against the Jews. They had charged him with prejudicing all men against the Jews and defiling the temple (Acts 21:27-29).

It was an extremely bad time for the voyage. The sailors knew this and had reconciled themselves to the fate of having to wait out the rest of the season in a safe harbor. It was during their run for such a harbor that they encountered hurricane winds (Acts 27:14,15). For two weeks they pitched and rolled. They couldn't catch even the faintest glimpse of sun by day or stars at night. All seemed hopeless (verse 20). That's when Paul gave them an encouraging word from God.

"Sirs, be of good cheer: for I believe God, that it shall be even as it was told me," Paul assured the seafarers (verse 25), as he unraveled the news that God's angel had appeared to him during the night, bringing a promise from God. Although the ship would be lost, no lives would be lost, and Paul would reach Rome in God's appointed time (verses 22-26).

It all turned out just as Paul reported. Paul never doubted that it would, for he believed God.

The faith in God's Word which Paul displayed on the high seas was typical of the confidence he had in God to do everything He promised. There was no credibility gap with God as far as Paul was concerned. For example, Paul was fully persuaded that God would keep him secure in salvation.

Salvation Is Forever

You can't fail to thrill to Paul's testimony in II Timothy 1:12: "I know whom I have believed, and am persuaded that he is able to keep that which I have committed unto him against that day." These are the words of a man who knew beyond a shadow of a doubt that salvation is forever.

Every Christian ought to be just as sure of stepping triumphantly into Heaven someday as Paul was. You see, Jesus Christ's keeping power hasn't diminished since Paul penned those comforting words, "he is able." As a matter of fact, our Lord's keeping power will never diminish.

The greatest threat to our assurance of eternal salvation as Christians comes from putting a question where God has put a declaration. We ask ourselves, "Am I able to keep that which I have committed unto him against that day?" when we ought to accept at face value the fact that "he is able."

If staying saved depended upon our efforts, none of us would stay saved for a day. The plain truth is, we are too feeble to walk uprightly, too lazy to pray fervently, and too worldly to desire Heaven. It is the Lord who takes us by the hand to enable us to walk in His ways. It is the Lord who kindles in our hearts the desire to pray. And it is the Lord who whets our appetite for the thousand sacred sweets of Zion's hill. Paul put it succinctly in Romans 7:18. Speaking for all Christians, he admitted, "How to perform that which is good I find not." But in Philippians 2:13 he turned the spotlight on divine sufficiency to perfect our salvation: "It is God which worketh in you both to will and to do of his good pleasure." So let's trust the Lord to keep us safe, and cooperate with His inworking to make us holy.

The Scriptures Are of God

Dwight L. Moody, the famous evangelist whose preaching moved thousands of Americans and Britishers to faith in Christ in the last quarter of the 19th century, cautioned Christians to use the whole Bible as the sword of the Spirit in the battles against the world, the flesh and the devil. Moody warned that it would be futile to do less. "You can't win battles with a broken sword," he explained.

Mr. Moody's words are even more urgently

needed today. When Moody sounded the charge to face the foe with the unbroken sword of the Spirit firmly in hand, there were few who denied that the whole Bible was the fully inspired, authoritative and trustworthy Word of God. Although liberalism was knocking at the doors of seminaries, denominational headquarters and churches, it had not yet entered more than a few. Today the picture is different; many denominations, seminaries, and churches have been victimized by liberalism. Entering as a robber, sometimes wearing this mask, sometimes another, liberalism has robbed many of their confidence in the Bible as God's Word.

The battle lines are drawn tightly now around several key terms, each of which is important in testing a person's orthodoxy.

Verbal inspiration. This means that the divine inspiration of the Scriptures extends even to the words of the original writing of the books of the Bible.

Plenary inspiration. This term signifies that all parts of the Bible are equally and fully inspired. For example, the book of Jonah is as divinely inspired as the Gospel of John.

Infallible. The Scriptures are wholly reliable.

Inerrant. The Scriptures will not lead us astray. They are without error.

There are profoundly significant implications to be derived from these definitions. Anyone who fails to believe that the Bible is God's Word from beginning to end, fully trustworthy and free of error, is either knowingly or unknowingly siding with the devil himself. After all, it was the devil who triggered doubt in Eve's mind about what God had said. He asked with a sneer, "Yea, hath God said . . .?" (Genesis 3:1).

Furthermore, if a person doubts God's Word, he cannot treasure its promises in the face of trials; he will not yield to its precepts and thereby lead a godly life; he cannot declare its message of good news with authority and joy; nor can he look forward with confidence to eternal life with God and His redeemed.

The Apostle Paul was a man of steel— unbending and strong—because he believed that God was the author of Scripture. Here's how Paul expressed this conviction: "All scripture is given by inspiration of God, and is profitable for doctrine, for reproof, for correction, for instruction in righteousness: That the man of God may be perfect, throughly furnished unto all good works" (II Timothy 3:16,17).

A literal translation of the first part of Paul's statement is, "All scripture God-breathed." Paul's view of Scripture, then, was this: God breathed out the Scriptures—every Scripture, all Scripture. Paul would have no difficulty subscribing to the verbal, plenary inspiration of the Bible.

Nor would he have any difficulty subscribing to the view that the Bible is infallible and inerrant. Paul recognized that the Scriptures have God for their source, and He described God as "faithful" (II Thessalonians 3:3) and incapable of lying (Titus 1:2). In other words, Paul recognized that God's Word bears the stamp of God's character. A God who is wholly perfect and perfectly holy would not deliver to man a written revelation which is less than faithful and flawless.

The Scriptures Are Powerful

Such confidence in God's Word on Paul's part led him to declare the Scriptures absolutely essential to salvation. In Romans 10:17 Paul wrote, "So then faith cometh by hearing, and hearing by the word of God." He informed Timothy that the holy Scriptures "are able to make thee wise unto salvation" (II Timothy 3:15). And he instructed the Philippians to hold forth "the word of life" (Philippians 2:16).

Paul was fully persuaded, too, that the Scriptures are indispensable to a life of godliness and effective Christian service. He advised the Ephesians that they must use the sword of the Spirit—the Word of God—in their warfare against Satan (Ephesians 6:17), and he advised Timothy that the Word indoctrinates, reproves, corrects, and instructs in righteousness in order to build us Christians up as mature, thoroughly equipped servants of God (II Timothy 3:16b,17).

Isn't there a great need today for a return to the Scriptures as the authoritative, fully reliable, and vitally necessary Word of God? Far too often a congregation settles for fluff 'n feathers sermons and entertainment instead of demanding sermons which expound and apply the Scriptures. And too often Christians accept religious experience as the standard for determining what is of God, when the Word of God is the only reliable standard for determining this.

Christian leaders are joining voices these days in declaring that we need a revival. They are right, we do need a revival—a Bible revival. Only when we restore the Bible to our full confidence will we be most like Paul—fully persuaded and committed to the God of the Word and to the Word of God.

Chapter 6

Hope: Planning on a Great Future

Hope. Is it alive and well on planet earth?

Environmentalists warn that earth is fast becoming a massive garbage pile. According to many of them, unless we stop polluting the environment and spoiling our natural resources we'll all suffocate under tons of refuse or choke to death on foul air.

Where is hope?

Ask many young men and women what hope they hold for the future of our civilization and they will reply with a terse, "None." They expect that only today is worth the living, for mankind seems bent on destroying himself.

Where is hope?

Following his transplant from South Vietnam to the United States when the communists overran South Vietnam, former South Vietnamese premier Nguyen Cao Ky spent many months traveling across the United States, speaking in city after city. His message? There is bound to be a third world war; military confrontation with communist powers is inevitable.

Where is hope?

Economists are worried about the future. Big cities are in financial trouble. New York City almost went under in 1975, and it isn't out of financial hot water yet. Detroit and other major cities are feeling the pains of a swelling deficit and shrinking available funds. Non-urban citizens fear that the big cities will eventually pull them down the drain with them.

Where is hope?

Hope Is in Christ

Christianity offers the only real hope for a world that seems to be falling apart. There is hope in Jesus Christ for all who trust in Him as Saviour and Lord. The Apostle Paul knew this, and it kept him on the top side of things. Neither persecution nor trials, which ganged up on him daily, make him feel like throwing in the towel and lament, "What's the use of following Christ? It's all so hopeless!" Not for a minute. Instead, Paul was triumphant in the hope that God had great things in store for him—and for every Christian.

Catch the spirit of hope in Paul's writings:

"So worship I the God of my fathers, believing all things which are written in the prophets: And have hope toward God . . .

that there shall be a resurrection of the dead" (Acts 24:14b,15).

"By whom also we have access by faith into this grace wherein we stand, and rejoice in hope of the glory of God" (Romans 5:2).

"Rejoicing in hope" (Romans 12:12).

"For whatsoever things were written aforetime were written for our learning, that we through patience and comfort of the scriptures might have hope. Now the God of hope fill you with all joy and peace in believing, that ye may abound in hope, through the power of the Holy Ghost" (Romans 15:4,13).

"We through the Spirit wait for the hope of righteousness by faith" (Galatians 5:5).

"Ye are called in one hope of your calling" (Ephesians 4:4).

"We give thanks to God and the Father of our Lord Jesus Christ . . . For the hope which is laid up for you in heaven" (Colossians 1:3,5).

"Christ in you, the hope of glory" (Colossians 1:27).

"But let us, who are of the day, be sober, putting on the breastplate of faith and love; and for an helmet, the hope of salvation" (I Thessalonians 5:8).

"Now our Lord Jesus Christ himself, and God, even our Father, which hath loved us, and hath given us everlasting consolation and good hope through grace, Comfort your hearts, and stablish you in every good word and work" (II Thessalonians 2:16,17).

"Paul, an apostle of Jesus Christ by the

commandment of God our Saviour, and Lord Jesus Christ, which is our hope" (I Timothy 1:1).

"In hope of eternal life, which God, that cannot lie, promised before the world began" (Titus 1:2).

"Looking for that blessed hope, and the glorious appearing of the great God and our Saviour Jesus Christ" (Titus 2:13).

"According to his mercy he saved us . . . That being justified by his grace, we should be made heirs according to the hope of eternal life" (Titus 3:5,7).

Convinced? Paul possessed a triumphant hope—a hope centered in Jesus Christ.

Hope for a Glorious Future

Christians who spend all their resources and energies to build a nest egg for this life are bound to be disappointed. It's an egg that won't hatch. You see, it's empty. There is nothing in this world that can give lasting satisfaction to those whose citizenship is in Heaven. Jesus warned, "Lay not up for yourselves treasures upon earth, where moth and rust doth corrupt, and where thieves break through and steal" (Matthew 6:19). And Paul cautioned Christians against setting our affection upon "things on the earth" (Colossians 3:2).

Both Jesus and Paul appealed to us to get our values straight—Heaven's treasures are worth far more than earth's treasures. "Lay up for yourselves treasures in heaven, where neither moth nor rust doth corrupt, and where thieves do not break through nor steal," Jesus commanded in Matthew 6:20. And Paul advised, "If ye then be risen with Christ, seek those things which are above, where Christ sitteth on the right hand of God. Set your affection on things above, not on things on the earth" (Colossians 3:1,2).

Someday Christians will leave earth behind, either by death or by being caught up alive at the rapture—the event when Christ comes in the air to remove His church from the earth. In either case our pilgrimage upon the earth will end and we shall embark upon a far better life—eternal life with our Lord. Then all of our amassed wealth, possessions and property will mean nothing. What will count is how well we invested our life and resources for the Lord's sake.

Paul spent his Christian life with these considerations in mind. He looked forward to Christ's coming. Writing to the Thessalonians, he confided, "The Lord himself shall descend from heaven with a shout, with the voice of the archangel, and with the trump of God: and the dead in Christ shall rise first: Then we which are alive and remain shall be caught up together with them in the clouds, to meet the Lord in the air; and so shall we ever be with the Lord" (I Thessalonians 4:16,17).

And if he died before the rapture, Paul was confident that he would go immediately into the presence of his Lord. He assured the Corinthians that "to be absent from the body" is "to be present with the Lord" (II Corinthians 5:8).

So, you see, Paul had a vibrant hope in Jesus Christ. But his hope embraced even more than leaving a hostile, sinful earth behind for the presence of Christ in Heaven. Paul fully expected to return with Christ to earth someday to reign.

A Better Day Ahead for Planet Earth

When the church is raptured, the earth will undergo all kinds of catastrophes. There will be wars, famines, earthquakes, pestilences, meteorite showers, vicious hailstorms, periods of intense darkness, tidal waves, scorching heat, uncontrollable grass and forest fires; and water sources will be contaminated (see Matthew 24:6,7,29; Revelation 6—16).

Demon activity will accelerate after the rapture. The earth will be filled with lawlessness. Atrocities will abound. Satanic religion will have a heyday. Governments will yield to the dictates of demonic powers. And in the midst of all this two degenerate leaders will emerge to take up key roles in world affairs. One will hold the reins of government over the territory once occupied by the Romans. The other will promote an apostate religion in Israel and cooperate with the first leader by directing the people's worship to him (Revelation 13).

This darkest hour of human history will be short-lived; it will last for only seven years (Daniel 9:27), terminating with the glorious return of Jesus Christ with His saints to the earth (Jude 14; Revelation 19). If you are a Christian, you will be among the saints Jesus Christ brings with Him.

When Christ returns to the earth, He will usher in a better day—the best the earth has known since the fall in the garden in Eden. Christ will destroy His enemies when he comes to earth (Revelation 19:15-18). He will dispose promptly of the two wicked leaders by casting them alive into the lake of fire (verse 20), and He will confine Satan to a thousand years in the bottomless pit (Revelation 20:2,3). Then He will set about to roll back the effects of the curse from nature and establish a kingdom of righteousness and justice.

Paul looked forward to this better day for our planet. He explained to the believers in Rome that nature itself is waiting patiently for Christ's kingdom: "The creature [creation] itself also shall be delivered from the bondage of corruption into the glorious liberty of the children of God. For we know that the whole creation groaneth and travaileth in pain until now" (Romans 8:21,22).

Knowing the Old Testament as he did, Paul understood that Messiah's kingdom will effect sweeping changes in nature and society. The desert areas will blossom like a rose and become productive. Nations will exchange their weapons for farm implements. The savage beasts will become gentle. Kingdom citizens will prosper and enjoy the fruits of their labor. Justice will prevail. Disease will be checked. Longevity will be the order of the day. And the Lord will be King over all the earth. (See Isaiah 9:6,7; 11; 35; 54:1-5; 65:18-23; Joel 2:21-26; Micah 4:3,4; Zechariah 14:9).

No Idle Wishing

Was Paul only kidding himself into thinking that a better day was coming? Some would say so, claiming that all the trials and persecution which befell him had squeezed him into an escapist's dream world. But they are wrong. Paul's hope was not spun from dreams; it was built with the fabric of faith—faith in God's Word. God had promised a glorious future for believers, so Paul lived "in hope of eternal life, which God, that cannot lie, promised" (Titus 1:2).

Of course, all the adversities Paul endured must have made his hope grow stronger. Each trial must have persuaded him to anchor his hope more firmly to the rock of Scripture. Charles Spurgeon made a helpful observation about this phenomenon: "When the anchor has been cast into a good ground the heavier the strain that comes on it, the deeper and firmer it holds."

We who are Christians ought to share Paul's hope, for Christ is in us "the hope of glory" (Colossians 1:27), and God's Word is just as true now as it was in Paul's time. Are we living in the sunshine of this hope, or are we so engrossed in the affairs of this life that a cloud of despair has settled over our heads? Let's look up, "for now is our salvation nearer than when we believed" (Romans 13:11).

And While We Wait . . .

The Apostle Paul maintained a proper balance in everything. He possessed a vibrant hope in the future God has planned for His own, but he didn't write off the present as a lost cause. Not for a minute. Paul worked vigorously to influence men and women for God while he waited for Christ to come for the church. And he exhorted Christians to "redeem" the time (Ephesians 5:16), pray for all men (I Timothy 2:1), be exemplary citizens (Romans 13), and hold forth "the word of life" (Philippians 2:16). It all adds up to plenty to do before the future arrives.

It is encouraging to see that Christians are becoming more involved in spreading their influence around. The "salt" is coming out of the shakers and many areas of society are feeling the effects. If this continues—and increases—we'll surely rescue many from a world that lies under divine judgment. In the process we may also preserve what remains of morality and decency in the twentieth century.

On the occasion of America's 200th birthday the *Rocky Mountain News* (Denver) posed a question to a number of recognized leaders. The question was what they believed to be the greatest threat to liberty in America and whether the nation can meet the challenge. Among the respondents was William L. Armstrong, United States representative from Colorado. His reply honored God, held forth hope, and exerted a Christian influence. Said Mr. Armstrong:

Americans have always acknowledged that human liberty is the gift of God. "Inalienable rights" are endowed by our "Creator," according to the Declaration of Independence. We pledge allegiance to the flag as citizens of "one nation under God" and our coins proclaim "In God We Trust." All too often, however, our actions counter these ritual expressions of faith. We Americans have come to depend more on ourselves and less on the Lord. So distinctions between right and wrong are blurred, standards of conduct degraded. Many of us permit "doing our own thing" to displace traditions of excellence, discipline and patriotism. We have created so many new government programs to solve problems that the very size of government itself has become a major problem, fostering unemployment and inflation, threatening to smother individuality and freedom. Faltering foreign policy, lagging defense, crime, drug abuse, pornography, official corruption, private apathy, these and other threats to liberty and survival symbolize how we have gradually forgotten the nation's Christian heritage. It is impossible to believe we can cope with such difficulties by purely human efforts. But now, a spiritual awakening of immense proportions is sweeping the country. Millions of Americans are accepting Jesus Christ as their personal Savior. By doing so, they gain assurance of their own salvation and afford a basis for solid optimism about saving the nation. I believe God will respond to the spiritualization of America as generously as He promised in 2 Chronicles 7:14: "Then if my people will humble themselves and pray, and search for me, and turn from their wicked ways, I will hear them from heaven and forgive their sins and heal their land." With this promise in mind, we can celebrate the Bicentennial with optimism and a renewed sense of confidence for the future of America.

There is much work to be done for the Lord while we wait for the realization of our Christian hope. Let's do more than hope to get on with it; let's get on with it *with hope.*

Chapter 7

The Love Principle

Love lies at the heart of Christianity. This sets Christianity apart from religions which operate on fear and superstition. Christianity proclaims God's love for sinners, revealed most clearly by His Son's death for sinners. Also, it provides a way for sinners to love God and others as they should. The fact is, when a person trusts in Christ as Saviour, the Holy Spirit infuses divine love into his heart (Romans 5:5; I John 3:14).

If you want to look at a miracle of divine love, look at Paul. God's love entered Paul's life with such forcefulness that his whole outlook was changed. Before believing in Christ his heart was filled with hatred. He lived for the moment when every Christian was either behind bars or six feet under. But after he became a believer in Christ his heart overflowed with divine love. He loved the Lord, he loved Christians, and he loved the lost—both Jews and Gentiles.

It is unfortunate that some persons have formed a distorted picture of the Apostle Paul. They cast him in the role of a bull-headed, insensitive "male chauvinist," who went steamrolling over anybody who got in his way and carried out a personal vendetta against women. Paul was quite the opposite, as the Scriptures plainly reveal.

Lots to Say about Love

Although we normally identify the Apostle John as "the apostle of love," it would not be amiss to ascribe the same title to Paul. His writings certainly rival John's in respect to the amount of teaching on love which they contain.

Paul taught in I Corinthians 13 about the noblest kind of love, *agape* love. This is love which finds its source in God. It is a self-sacrificing love. It puts another's interests ahead of personal interests. It is generated by the Holy Spirit and outshines all other Christian virtues, as important as they are. There is no substitute for *agape* love.

Without this kind of love eloquent speaking in a variety of languages is pointless (verse 1). Preaching at its best without love falls flat, and spectacular faith without love amounts to nothing, according to verse 2. A person may even perform magnificent humanitarian acts, but if these are not motivated by love they hold no spiritual value (verse 3a). Why, a person may go so far as to offer his body to be burned for the sake of a cause he believes in, but if love—*agape* love—isn't back of it all the act is worthless.

We Christians need to stop long enough once in a while to examine what we profess to be doing for the Lord. It's so easy to say what we are expected to say without having love as the motive behind our words. Testimonies may be offered, Sunday School lessons taught, an outline of salvation presented, and sermons preached without love. Quite possibly a Christian may care a great deal for speaking and not care at all for those to whom he speaks. If love doesn't undergird the words, there will be no eternal reward for speaking them.

First Corinthians 13 ought to set some persons back on their heels. For example, the person who witnesses without love. You may know the type. He seems bent on buttonholing sinners simply to wring a confession of faith from them in order for him to boast about how many souls he won to the Lord in a given week.

Or there's the pastor (fortunately there aren't many like him) who brags at the Monday morning pastors' breakfast, "I really let my people have it yesterday. I threw the whole book at them—really nailed their hides to the wall. What a sermon!"

Also we need to ask whether we are filling roles of Christian work because others expect us to do so. "What would Brother Jones think of me," we ask, "if I refused to teach fifth-grade boys?"

We can drift so easily into the rut of

performing mere perfunctory service if we are not careful. We can lose our love for others, or much of our love for the Lord, and function in a climate of cold professionalism. As you may recall, this happened to the Christians at Ephesus. When Paul wrote his epistle to them he counseled them to "walk in love" (Ephesians 5:2). But by the end of the century the church at Ephesus had left its first love (Revelation 2:4). It was still holding to orthodox teaching. It was still performing works. But its love had grown cold.

Someone has observed that the last three letters of "service" spell "ice," and some Christians need defrosting. The Ephesian believers at the close of the first century needed defrosting. What about us twentieth-century Christians?

Let's return now to the great love chapter—I Corinthians 13—for a further look at what Paul had to say about this supreme characteristic, love.

Love displays patience. "Love suffereth long," Paul told the Corinthians. Interestingly, the word for "suffereth" suggests being patient with people. The New Testament supplies a different word for being patient with circumstances. The Corinthians needed this explanation, for they were an impatient group. They were too quick to grumble and rumble among themselves. Unable to settle their disputes peaceably, they carted one another off to the local judge (I Corinthians 6:1).

Paul's word about patience with people is

needed today. Far too often a new Christian's morale is demolished because some older Christian cannot wait for the Holy Spirit to apply the Word to certain areas of the new Christian's life. The new Christian is severely censured for carrying over certain habits or dress styles into the new life. The criticism he receives, which hasn't been offered in love, pains the new believer and either drives him away from the church or dulls his desire for more than minimal Christian fellowship.

It's a good thing surgeons don't *operate* like impatient Christians. A surgeon prepares a patient for surgery—gently, thoroughly. He never removes an offending organ from the patient's body without having administered a proper anesthetic. His goal is to free the patient of his ailment with a minimum amount of pain being experienced by the patient. Unlike the surgeon, the hypercritical and impatient older Christian launches a verbal assault against the new believer, knocks him off his feet, and proceeds to extract from him the offending taboos. It does not seem to matter how much pain he inflicts upon the new believer during the operation. Nor does it seem to matter whether the new Christian pulls through.

In his letter to the Galatians Paul advised "spiritual" Christians to show their love for a brother "overtaken in a fault" by restoring him to a right relationship with Christ. He urged them to carry out the assignment "in the spirit of meekness; considering thyself, lest thou also be tempted" (Galatians 6:1).

Isn't Paul's way best? It calls for *agape* love, which displays patience toward another.

When we are tempted to become impatient with others and critical, let's think about it: The only bit that can bridle the tongue is a bit of love.

There's a strange phenomenon that occurs in a number of marriages. Have you observed it? During the first year of wedded life a husband and wife are blind to each other's faults. The wife shows excitement about picking up her husband's socks and washing his shirts. She tells him how wonderful it is to have her very own man to care for. The husband, in turn, never criticizes his wife's cooking. His eyes scale the table's helpings of instant hash and undercooked TV dinners with all the adventurous delight a mountain climbing team experiences upon reaching the top of Mount McKinley.

Then the second year of marriage comes along. By now the wife is complaining about a certain backache she gets when she bends over to pick up socks or do the laundry. And the husband is suggesting that his wife find out from his mother how to make the good things he enjoyed eating when he was growing up.

The third year inaugurates the war. The wife screams at her husband that he is the sloppiest, laziest person she ever met. She supports her accusation by pointing vindictively at yesterday's socks still lying at the foot of the bed where he had dropped them. She asks sarcastically if he knows what a laundry basket is for. When he says he does know what it is for, she yells, "That's for sure; you must drop two shirts a day there for me to wash. Can't you at least make sure a shirt needs to be cleaned before you dump it in the laundry basket? Or do you just delight to make my bad back act up?"

And what about meal times? These provide an opportunity for the husband to bring out the heavy artillery. He accuses his wife of trying to end his life by frostbite by serving so many frozen foods. He indicts her for contributing to the pollution of the environment by piling garbage on the dinner table. Then comes the lowest blow of all; he tells his wife that she must have inspired the author of the *I Hate to Cook Cookbook* to write her book.

What has happened? Love has grown cold, and in the process faults have loomed large. As a result, another marriage is headed for the divorce court.

If we practice *agape* love, we'll be patient with one another—in our homes and in our churches.

Love displays kindness. Paul told the Corinthians in I Corinthians 13:4 that "love is kind." Christians ought to be kind to one another (Ephesians 4:32). We should avoid saying and doing anything that will hurt another person. A pat on the back, rather than a club over the head, will help a person to grow taller in Christ and go farther for Christ in the long run.

Love isn't envious. Paul wrote, "Love envieth not" (I Corinthians 13:4). What a difference this *agape* love makes in personal and church relationships! Instead of resenting the good that comes into another's life, including job promotions and election to church offices, a loving Christian rejoices with the recipients.

Love doesn't brag. "Love vaunteth not itself, is not puffed up," Paul told the church at Corinth (verse 4). This is in keeping with our Lord's teaching to His disciples that the greatest follower He has is the servant of all (Mark 10:44). Instead of boasting about his own accomplishments, a loving Christian will invest his time in singing the praises of the Lord.

Love is gracious. Paul informed his readers that "love doth not behave itself unseemly" (I Corinthians 13:5). A showoff and a rude person bring disgrace to themselves. When a Christian acts in either of these ways, he disgraces his Lord and shows that he is bankrupt concerning *agape* love.

Love is meek. Paul taught that love "seeketh not her own" (verse 5). When a Christian pulls out all the stops to advance his own interests, he needs to face the fact that he does not possess *agape* love.

Love never flies off the handle. Also in verse 5 Paul insisted that love never gets fed up with people—"is not easily provoked." Don't go around blaming everyone for the "rotten shape of things." If you do, according to Paul, you simply reveal that you have not love.

Love doesn't nurse a grudge. Paul employed an accountant's word when he wrote that love "thinketh" no evil. The word means to enter something into an account so that it will be remembered. A Christian who goes around with a chip on his shoulder and a grudge in his heart, is keeping accounts which should have been canceled. Love—*agape* love—doesn't keep records of personal offences.

Love is never happy about wrongdoing. Love, according to Paul, "rejoiceth not in iniquity" (verse 6). Instead, it "rejoiceth in the truth" (verse 6). There is something woefully wrong with us if we get a kick out of hearing that a Christian has fallen into sin. Love grieves for the backslidden.

Love endures everything. According to verse 7, love "beareth all things." No adverse criticism or tough circumstances can thwart a loving Christian from doing God's will in behalf of others. Love will keep him at his post when even his closest friends tell him it just isn't worth the dedication.

Love believes God and hopes for the best. Paul advised the Corinthians of these things in verse 7. It is *agape* love that keeps us confident that God will keep His word. It will not let us doubt His fairness or His ability to work in the lives of others even though their present conduct seems unpromising.

Love is permanent. Agape love will stand the test of time. It will weather the storms. It will come through with flying colors. This is the message Paul inscribed in the closing verses of I Corinthians 13. So if you want to have eternity in what you do, do everything in an attitude of love.

Paul Showed Love

Paul didn't lecture on love without living with love in his heart. He showed how greatly he loved the lost by traveling the length and breadth of the civilized world to share with men everywhere the message of God's saving grace. "The love of Christ constraineth us," he wrote in II Corinthians 5:14, explaining why he was serving faithfully as an ambassador of Christ. Christ's love urged him forward to preach the gospel to the lost.

Paul's love for the lost was so great that he wished himself accursed from Christ if that might help to bring the Jews to faith in Jesus Christ (Romans 9:1-3). His heart's desire was to see them come to Christ for salvation (Romans 10:1).

Once in a while we learn of a situation in which a parent shows sacrificial love for a son or daughter. The incident helps us to understand Paul's willingness to suffer loss of salvation if it were possible in order to win others to Christ. For example, some time ago a young woman learned that she needed a kidney transplant. Her mother stepped forward to offer one of her kidneys for the transplant. The doctors agreed, and the mother put her life on the operating table so that her daughter might have life. Fortunately, both mother and daughter came through the surgery successfully.

If you are a parent, you know that you

would rather suffer instead of your child. If you learned that your child had an incurable disease, you would wish that it were possible for you to bear the disease for your child. This compares in some measure to Paul's wish that he could exchange places with the Jews so that they might have eternal life. What love!

And Paul loved Christians too. He ended his first letter to the Christians with "My love be with you all in Christ Jesus" (I Corinthians 16:24). In II Corinthians 11:28 he alluded to the care that he had for all the churches (he was as concerned for them as a devoted mother is for the well-being of her children). He told the Philippians that he longed for them with Christlike compassion (Philippians 1:8). He informed the Galatians that he was experiencing travail as he longed to see them become mature believers in Christ (Galatians 4:19). And he told the Thessalonians how he was praying night and day for them. He was beseeching God to increase their love for one another and for all men (I Thessalonians 3:10-12).

There's no doubt about it, Paul possessed and displayed *agape* love. He deserves to be regarded as a man who loved the Lord and the Lord's people and not as the insensitive, headstrong dictator some people make him out to have been. We would do well to have and show the same love. Then we would fulfill Jesus' prediction: "By this shall all men know that ye are my disciples, if ye have love one to another" (John 13:35).

Chapter 8

Man of Prayer

The Lord introduced Paul—His trophy of grace—to the Christian community by telling Ananias: "Behold, he prayeth" (Acts 9:11). Our Lord's words to Ananias reveal two important facts: first, when a believer prays, God listens; second, from the very beginning of his Christian life Paul was a man of prayer. Both of these facts ought to encourage us Christians to pray confidently and consistently.

Obviously, a newly saved person may give himself wholeheartedly to prayer following his conversion only to slack off later on. But this was not Paul's experience. He prayed earnestly and consistently throughout his earthly pilgrimage. Furthermore, he left the challenge to us to "pray without ceasing" (I Thessalonians 5:17).

Paul's Prayer Times

The New Testament records a number of occasions when Paul prayed. Knowing when he prayed will help us to recognize situations when we ought to give ourselves to prayer.

Undoubtedly Paul must have prayed often during the three years of his seclusion in the desert region of Arabia (Galatians 1:15-18). As we noted in an earlier chapter, this was a period when God was instructing Paul in the doctrines of grace prior to his public ministry as an apostle.

Also, it isn't stretching matters too far to suppose that Paul engaged in prayer just before the church at Antioch commissioned him and Barnabas for missionary service. In all probability Paul had been praying that the believers would recognize God's call upon his life for this very purpose. The event is described for us in Acts 13:1-3: "Now there were in the church that was at Antioch certain prophets and teachers ... As they ministered to the Lord, and fasted, the Holy Ghost said, Separate me Barnabas and Saul for the work whereunto I have called them. And when they had fasted and prayed, and laid their hands on them, they sent them away."

As a missionary, Paul engaged in prayer to invoke God's blessings upon his labor. Acts 14 tells us that when Paul and Barnabas had confirmed the souls of the disciples in Lystra, Iconium, and Pisidian Antioch, had exhorted them to continue in the faith, had forewarned them of coming tribulation, and had ordained elders in every church, they prayed with fasting, and commended the believers to the Lord (verses 21-23).

In Philippi Paul and another missionary, Silas, saw people saved and baptized. But they also fell heir to some rough treatment. They were beaten and slammed into jail. But they didn't wring their hands and moan, "God must not answer prayer. Look where serving the Lord has got us." No, indeed! At Midnight Paul—man of prayer—and his companion "prayed, and sang praises unto God" (Acts 16:25).

Of course, God sprang Paul and Silas from jail, for He had further plans for Paul—plans that would take Paul to other cities and countries for the sake of the gospel. One of those places was Ephesus, where God raised up a host of believers as Paul preached and taught for two years.

Later, Paul's journeying led him back to the vicinity of Ephesus, to Miletus, a town to the south of Ephesus. From there Paul summoned the elders of the church at Ephesus to meet with him. He delivered a touching message to them, reminding them of the ministry he had performed among them and charging them to take great care to feed the flock and watch out for false teachers. Following this address, Paul "kneeled down, and prayed with them all" (Acts 20:36).

The book of Acts closes with another reference to Paul praying. This time Paul was a prisoner under armed escort en route to Rome to stand trial. A number of Christians found out that Paul was in the area, so they traveled to meet him. When Paul saw them "he thanked God, and took courage" (Acts 28:15).

Second Corinthians 12:7-9 points to another instance when Paul prayed. The occasion preceded the writing of II Corinthians by about fourteen years. At that time, a severe trial had settled down on Paul, and Paul prayed three times for God to remove the affliction. In this case the Lord did not do what Paul asked Him to do, namely, remove the affliction. Rather He supplied enough grace for Paul to endure the affliction victoriously.

Finally, we learn from Paul's second letter to Timothy that Paul was still practicing prayer at the close of his life. Second Timothy was Paul's final New Testament letter, written from a dismal Roman dungeon, with the apostle expecting to be executed before long. We catch the spirit of victory in Paul's life as we receive the testimony of this man of prayer. Paul assured Timothy that he was remembering him in his "prayers night and day" (II Timothy 1:3).

We can learn to pray when we encounter situations somewhat similar to Paul's. We can pray when we are about to accept a new service assignment. It's true, we can do more than pray, but we cannot do anything well until we have prayed. We can pray while we serve the Lord, asking Him to undergird our ministry with His power. We can pray when tough times come along, threatening to knock us off-balance. We can pray when we say good-bye to Christian friends as we depart for a new location, and we can pray when God brings new Christian friends into our life. Finally, we can pray when we come down to the close of our life. We can pray from start to finish—from our conversion to Christ until we see Him face to face.

"Pray without ceasing."

Paul Prayed for Others

There is a great deal of mindless praying among us Christians. That is, we are often guilty of praying with our speech in high gear while our minds are in neutral. We fall victim to the tendency to offer lazy cliches: "Lord, be with all the missionaries." "Bless the Millers." "Just be with our young people in their meeting next Sunday." "Lord, lead, guide and direct us." This is how we pray far too often. Wouldn't it be better to pray with understanding when we pray for others?

Examine your personal praying for a moment, not just the prayers you offer in Prayer Meeting or when the pastor calls on you to lead or close a meeting in prayer but also the prayers you offer in the quiet of your home. Do you focus divine attention on your own wants and needs to the exclusion of asking God to meet the needs of others? Do you maintain a prayer list—if not written, at least mental—in which you include requests for the salvation of unsaved persons and the spiritual growth of fellow Christians?

All of us can improve our prayer life by following the pattern Paul set as he prayed for sinners to be saved (Romans 10:1) and for saints to be sanctified and empowered.

When Paul thought about the Christians throughout the Roman empire, he gave thanks to God for them. Do you give thanks for the Christians you know? For all of them?

Paul wrote in I Corinthians 1:4, "I thank my God always on your behalf, for the grace of God which is given you by Jesus Christ."

He informed the Ephesians, "Wherefore I also, after I heard of your faith in the Lord Jesus, and love unto all the saints, Cease not to give thanks for you, making mention of you in my prayers" (Ephesians 1:15,16).

He told the Philippians, "I thank my God upon every remembrance of you" (Phillippians 1:3).

He wrote to the Thessalonians, "We give thanks to God always for you all, making mention of you in our prayers" (I Thessalonians 1:2).

Not only did Paul give thanks for his fellow Christians, he also prayed for their spiritual growth. One of these prayers is found in chapters 1 and 3 of Ephesians with chapter 2 dividing it into two sections. The content of the prayer serves as a classic example of how we ought to pray for one another as Christians. Basically, the prayer petitions the Lord to grant four requests in behalf of the Ephesian Christians.

Paul petitioned the Lord to give "the spirit of wisdom and revelation in the knowledge of him" (Ephesians 1:17). This suggests getting to know the Lord better on the basis of His self-revelation. For us Christians to know the Lord better we must understand His revelation—the Scriptures.

On the surface it may not seem very important to pray in this manner for others. Yet, there are many unscriptural views of Christ circulating today. It is absolutely urgent, therefore, that our fellow believers form a view of Him that is based solidly on the Bible. There simply is no way for them to get to know the Lord better without getting to know His Word better.

Also, Paul prayed that the Ephesians would "know what is the hope of his calling, and what the riches of the glory of his inheritance in the saints" (verse 18). He wanted them to enjoy the same thrilling hope and sense of inheritance he enjoyed. He wanted them to lay hold on God's promises and expect to be conformed to the image of Christ someday (Romans 8:29) and to bask in the glory they would share with Christ in that day.

Appropriate for our modern times? You know it is. How good it is for us Christians to realize that God will perfect His will on our behalf and bring us into full possession of our inheritance through Christ. This lifts our spirits and helps us to live with a feeling of triumphant anticipation in our hearts and a glad song on our lips.

"And what is the exceeding greatness of his power to us-ward who believe," Paul continued in Ephesians 1:19. He longed to see

God's power operating uninhibitedly among the believers at Ephesus. This power was demonstrated clearly in God's great act of raising Jesus Christ from the dead to sit at God's right hand and exercise lordship over the church (verses 20-23).

It's good to pray for other Christians in this way. What Christian cannot welcome a greater appreciation of God's almighty and available power? Such an appreciation of divine power persuades us to trust Him to strengthen us for whatever duties He gives us to perform. If God could raise His Son from the dead—and He did—nothing is too hard for Him. Our weaknesses are only His opportunities to display omnipotence.

Finally, Paul prayed in Ephesians 3 that as the Christians at Ephesus grew stronger spiritually and became better acquainted with Jesus Christ they would "be able to comprehend with all saints what is the breadth, and length, and depth, and height; and to know the love of Christ, which passeth knowledge" (verses 18,19).

Do you realize what Paul was asking God to do? He was asking Him to do what seemed to be impossible—to give the Ephesians a grasp for the full dimensions of Christ's love. He knew that he was asking for what appeared to be impossible, for he followed up this request by referring to God as the One "that is able to do exceeding abundantly above all that we ask or think, according to the power that worketh in us" (verse 20).

God can make us know the unknowable—"the love of Christ, which passeth knowledge." Oh, we cannot figure out why He loves us. We cannot fathom the depths of His love. We cannot chart its boundaries. But in the recesses of our inner man we can know the love of Christ. We can know that it is broad enough to include a world of sinners, long enough to span the centuries and eternity, deep enough to reach down to the foulest sinner, and high enough to be out of reach to any foe that tries to rob us of it. And we can know it by personally experiencing it.

Asking God to give our fellow Christians this kind of knowledge makes sense, for it is the best gift God gives to those who love Him.

Indeed, Paul was a man of prayer. He prayed consistently and intelligently. He prayed with faith, and he prayed with compassion. Let's follow his example.

Lord, what a change within us one short hour
Spent in Thy presence will avail to make!
What heavy burdens from our bosoms take!
What parched grounds refresh, as with a shower!
Why, therefore, should we do ourselves this wrong
Or others—that we are not always strong?
That we are ever overborne with care,
That we should ever weak or heartless be,
Anxious or troubled, when with us is prayer,
And joy and strength and courage are with Thee?

—Richard C. Trench

Chapter 9

Defender
of the Faith

"No one has a corner on truth," we are told. But how about God? Surely He has a corner on truth, for He cannot lie (Titus 1:2).

Paul believed that what God had revealed by His Spirit was truth—truth worth defending. He acknowledged this in Philippians 1:17 by declaring, "I am set for the defence of the gospel." And he had plenty of opportunities in his missionary career to show that this declaration wasn't just so much hot air.

It Happened in Athens

For example, there was the time he defended the gospel on Athens' Mars Hill. Not an easy task, for Mars Hill was the focal point of Greek intellectual life. It was the site of the Areopagus, the Greek supreme court, where important decisions were formed affecting Greek culture. Some writers suggest that Paul delivered his defense of the gospel from the white Stone of Shame reserved for defendants.

Not only was Athens an intellectual center, it was also a religious center. Religious shrines gleamed everywhere in the Athenian sun, for the people bowed down to numerous pagan deities in addition to Mars and Athene, for whom two elaborate temples had been erected.

So there stood Paul in the midst of the supreme court, surrounded by philosophers, jurists, and religious devotees. It was indeed a lonely spot—a hot spot—for the little giant of faith, Paul. The scene is reminiscent of Daniel in the lions' den. It is reminiscent, too, of another hill-top encounter—Elijah's encounter with hundreds of false prophets on Mount Carmel (I Kings 18:20-40). On that memorable occasion pure and undefiled religion opposed corrupt and devilish religion. Alone, Elijah stood his ground for Jehovah and served notice that Jehovah is the only true God.

Of course God was alongside Paul in the Areopagus. If Paul stood on the Stone of Shame to deliver his defense of the gospel, he had no reason to be ashamed, for all the power of the Creator of the universe was at his disposal. Is it any wonder what happened? At the close of the apostle's address some of Athen's important decision-makers made the most important decision of all—they believed on Jesus Christ as Lord and Saviour (Acts 17:34).

If you could put a modern—day, neo-liberal theologian in a time capsule, shoot him back through time to Mars Hill in the first century, and plop him down on the Stone of Shame right smack in the middle of the Areopagus to tell what he believed, it would be shocking to hear his speech. He would likely congratulate the gathering on their interest in religion and explain that he, too, was a seeker of truth. Perhaps he would encourage them to seek an encounter with the Ground of All Being through nature and the study of religious history. He might go so far as to suggest that they add to their religious exercises a study of Old Testament prophets and Jesus to discover truth in their revelations concerning "God." About halfway through his address you would want to get him back into the time capsule as fast as possible and recall him. After all, to let him continue would be contributing to the further ignorance of the audience.

When Paul spoke to the assembly on Mars Hill he had something to say—something authoritative and worthwhile. He had Christ to proclaim.

Paul told the assembled greats that they were very religious but ignorant of the one true God. Then he declared this One to them. He assured them that God is all-powerful—the Creator of all things, all-wise—the Lord of the universe, all-gracious—the Giver and Sustainer of life, all-loving—available to all who seek Him, and all-righteous—unalterably opposed to sin. In his concluding remarks he called upon the Areopagus to repent, warning them of sure judgment at the hands of God's risen Son if they failed to avail themselves of God's offer of mercy. "God . . . now commandeth all men every where to repent," Paul announced, "Because he hath appointed a day, in the which he will judge the world in righteousness by that man whom he hath ordained; whereof he hath given assurance unto all men, in that he hath raised him from the dead" (Acts 17:30,31).

Doesn't it fortify your faith and set the joy bells ringing in your heart to receive this confident declaration from Paul? It ought to, for Paul's declaration underscores the unchanging fact that Jesus Christ rose bodily from the grave and will have the final say regarding human destiny. What a victorious, sovereign Lord!

What Paul declared about Christ on Mars Hill was the dominant theme of his teaching. Follow his missionary career through the book of Acts, and you will hear him preach the risen Christ over and over again. Read his epistles, and you will find him writing about the risen Christ over and over again. Here are just a few excerpts from those epistles.

"Declared to be the Son of God with power, according to the spirit of holiness, by the resurrection from the dead" (Romans 1:4).

"Who was delivered for our offences, and was raised again for our justification" (Romans 4:25).

"Christ was raised up from the dead by the glory of the Father . . . Christ being raised from the dead dieth no more" (Romans 6:4,9).

"It is Christ that died, yea rather, that is

risen again, who is even at the right hand of God" (Romans 8:34).

"God hath both raised up the Lord, and will raise up us by his own power" (I Corinthians 6:14).

"Now is Christ risen from the dead" (I Corinthians 15:20).

"Knowing that he which raised up the Lord Jesus shall raise up us also by Jesus" (II Corinthians 4:14).

"He raised him from the dead, and set him at his own right hand in the heavenly places" (Ephesians 1:20).

"God . . . hath raised him from the dead" (Colossians 2:12).

"And to wait for his Son from heaven, whom he raised from the dead, even Jesus, which delivered us from the wrath to come" (I Thessalonians 1:10).

"Remember that Jesus Christ of the seed of David was raised from the dead according to my gospel" (II Timothy 2:8).

There's no doubt about it, Paul believed and proclaimed Jesus Christ as the Son of God who arose victoriously after suffering for our sins on Calvary. This is the belief we must hold. It is the truth we must proclaim. Let's stand firm for the faith which looks beyond the cross to an open tomb and living Saviour.

No Compromise

In preaching the risen Saviour Paul made it clear that salvation is all a work of grace. Sinners are saved solely on the basis of Christ's substitutionary death and glorious resurrection. "Christ died for our sins," Paul preached. "He was buried, and . . . rose again," he declared. (I Corinthians 15:3,4) Here's what he communicated to the Christians at Rome: "The word is nigh thee, even in thy mouth, and in thy heart: that is, the word of faith, which we preach; that if thou shalt confess with thy mouth the Lord Jesus, and shalt believe in thine heart that God hath raised him from the dead, thou shalt be saved" (Romans 10:8,9).

Nothing crept into Paul's message of salvation to suggest that man has something to contribute to God's saving grace. Writing about salvation by grace to the Ephesians, Paul emphasized that salvation is "not of works, lest any man should boast" (Ephesians 2:9). This was what Paul preached to the Gentiles. And it wasn't long before it brought him into sharp controversy with Judaizers.

The Epistle to the Galatians tells the story. After Paul had departed from the province of Galatia, leaving behind him a string of churches comprised of saved-by-grace Gentiles, Judaizers swept into the churches and upset the theological apple cart.

"You Gentiles can't be fully saved or live pleasing to God unless you receive the rite of circumcision and live as Jews under the Mosaic law," the Judaizers insisted. Their personality and arguments were so convincing that many Galatians embraced lawkeeping as the way to full salvation. Paul was sure they had been "bewitched" by the false teachers (Galatians 3:1). So he wrote Galatians to set them straight—to bring them back to the assurance of salvation by grace alone.

In Galatians, chapter 2, Paul recounted an incident that had occurred some time prior to writing the epistle. He had gone to Jerusalem to defend the gospel of grace before Judaizers in the presence of Hebrew Christian leaders. According to Paul, the occasion resulted in a great victory for the gospel of grace. Although the Judaizers didn't like it, the council at Jerusalem concluded that Gentiles could come into perfect standing in God's sight apart from circumcision and lawkeeping. They did not have to become Jews at all. They could be saved just as Jews were saved—by grace (see Acts 15).

An interesting feature of the council meeting at Jerusalem was the appearance of a saved Gentile—Titus—whom Paul had brought with him as exhibit A of the power of God among the Gentiles. Truly, Paul was a masterful defender of the faith!

He sounded a call to the Galatians to rid themselves of Judaistic influence and return to the freedom with which Christ had set them free when first they had believed on Him (Galatians 5:1).

We need to stand firm for the faith today. The all-encompassing religious attitudes of first-century Athens are still around, and they are just as empty and ignorant of the truth as ever. Also, the Judaizing spirit manages to pervade the thinking of more than a few professing Christians. We must resist any teaching that detracts from the Scriptural declaration of Christ as the only Saviour, God's crucified and risen Son. We dare not compromise our conviction for a moment that our only hope is salvation by grace.

Long before Paul preached to the Gentiles that salvation is found only in the Lord Jesus Christ, another messenger from God pleaded with the Gentiles to turn to God. His name was Jonah.

You remember, don't you, that Jonah was reluctant at first to go to the Gentiles? But God used a great fish to make him willing to go.

Interestingly, after three days and three nights in the belly of the fish—when Jonah was at last willing to go to the Gentiles with God's message—he acknowledged, "Salvation is of the Lord" (Jonah 2:9). It was then that "the Lord spake unto the fish, and it vomited out Jonah upon the dry land" (verse 10).

Someone has commented about that extraordinary outcome by observing, "Jonah was a believer, and the great fish was a liberal. When Jonah declared, 'Salvation is of the Lord,' the great fish decided, 'I can't stomach this,' and therefore cast out Jonah."

Although the comment contains basic flaws, it does point accurately to the lack of appreciation liberal religionists have for the gospel. To be sure, the same persons will oppose us Christians as we proclaim the gospel. Nevertheless, let us proclaim it and defend it with as much fervor and courage as Paul showed throughout his years of Christian service.

Chapter 10

Fatherly Concern

There is something wonderful about a good father-son relationship. It's a relationship in which the father loves his son, provides for him, instills in him a sense of decency, outfits him with moral and spiritual values, challenges him to be honest and dependable, and helps him to become a productive member of society—a credit to his father and to the Lord. The son, in turn, loves his father, trusts him, respects and obeys him, and develops his God-given talents, gifts and skills to the maximum.

The Apostle Paul maintained a spiritual father-son relationship with two choice young servants of God—Timothy and Titus. Both were pastors when Paul wrote his New Testament letters to them. Apparently he had been instrumental in winning each of them to the Saviour, for he refers to them affectionately as his sons in the faith (I Timothy 1:2; Titus 1:4).

Timothy was won to Christ when Paul came to Lystra, Timothy's home town, on his second missionary journey (Acts 16:1). The son of a Greek father and Jewish mother, Timothy had received a rich indoctrination in the Old Testament Scriptures before he heard the gospel. The written Word, then, had prepared him well for the message of salvation Paul brought to him. Paul took Timothy under his wing and permitted him to join him in his missionary travels. Timothy accompanied Paul through Macedonia, was with him in Corinth, and went along with him on his last visit to Jerusalem. He became the pastor of the church at Ephesus.

Titus accompanied Paul from Antioch to Jerusalem to be exhibit A in defense of the gospel of grace, as we noted in the last chapter. He was obviously a Gentile, whom Paul took along on some of his travels. Indeed Paul placed a great deal of trust in Titus, for it seems he dispatched him to Corinth with the first epistle to the Corinthians (II Corinthians 7:6-8). He trusted Titus to stimulate the Corinthian church to put its house in order, and to take charge of the collection there for the relief of the poor saints in Jerusalem. Eventually, Titus became the pastor of the church in Crete. Paul wanted Titus to visit him when he was wintering in Nicopolis, and later when the apostle was imprisoned in Rome Titus was with him as a faithful friend. Our last information about Titus indicates that Paul sent him from Rome to the province of Dalmatia (Yugoslavia).

You can see, then, that Paul was closely bound to Timothy and Titus in Christian fellowship. When he called each of them his son in the faith he was not using the term loosely; he truly regarded each of them with warm, paternal affection. He viewed himself as their spiritual father, and in his letters to them he displayed a great deal of fatherly concern for them.

A Pat on the Back

Timothy seems to have been subject to discouragement and even self-pity from time to time. He must have been a rather sensitive young man, who found the pastorate at Ephesus more than a little difficult. False teachers were invading the ranks of the faithful, worldly attitudes were settling into the thinking of some, and a few were discrediting Timothy's effectiveness because he was youthful. Some Bible teachers insist that a combination of these adverse circumstances had resulted in a case of ulcers for Pastor Timothy. They support their conclusion by pointing to Paul's advice to Timothy to "use a little wine for thy stomach's sake and thine often infirmities" (I Timothy 5:23).

Knowing Timothy's difficulties and disposition, Paul took him aside from the pressures of the pastorate long enough to nurse his hurts and apply the balm of encouragement. As Timothy read each of the two letters from Paul he gained the benefit of fatherly counsel. He must have returned to the work of the ministry refreshed and optimistic.

It's helpful to see how the veteran missionary, Paul, lifted the drooping spirit of his "own son in the faith." What we learn from his counseling will help us to avoid blundering our way through a similar situation in which we are called upon to encourage a fellow Christian.

First—and this is so important—Paul didn't try to make Timothy believe that there really wasn't a problem at all. He acknowledged the existence of false teachers in Ephesus. He recognized that these wolves in sheep's clothing posed a threat to Timothy's ministry. He identified these false teachers as legalists (I Timothy 1:6,7), followers of demons (4:1), liars and hypocrites (4:2), men who were corrupt and destitute of the truth (6:5).

Having agreed that this problem existed, Paul proceeded to draw Timothy's attention to the positive side of things. Timothy's strength lay in the resources of God (I Timothy 1:2,17a; II Timothy 1:2,7; 2:1). Timothy could draw encouragement from the fact that God had called and prepared him for the work of the ministry (I Timothy 1:18; 4:14; 6:20; II Timothy 1:6,14).

Then Paul patted Timothy on the back and said, in effect, "Timothy, get with it. Get into the fight of faith and give it all you've got. And you've got a lot to give, for God has seen to that" (I Timothy 1:18; 4:16; 5:21; 6:11-14; II Timothy 1:8; 2:3,22; 3:14; 4:2,3,5).

If we minimize the problems another Christian faces and suggest that he is just looking for sympathy, we simply aren't helping him—that is, if there are problems confronting him. It is far better to admit that the Christian life does have plenty of problems but encourage the troubled Christian to draw upon the resources of God who is greater than all the problems. Once his attention is riveted on God's resources we can pat him on the back and advise him to stay with the fight.

Paul encouraged Titus too.

Titus pastored on the island of Crete. It wasn't exactly the ideal pastorate. The people who lived on Crete had a reputation—a bad reputation. One of their own poets had described them as lazy gluttons, who spent their days telling lies and acting in a bestial manner (see Titus 1:12,13). And to top off the situation there were false teachers to contend with—plenty of them. Paul recognized this. He wrote, "There are many unruly and vain talkers and deceivers, specially they of the circumcision" (Titus 1:10).

Titus had a big job on his hands, but it was a job Paul was sure he could accomplish.

After all, he had left Titus on the island of Crete to set church matters in order (Titus 1:5). This proved to Titus that he had Paul's full confidence. In his letter to Titus he reinforced this confidence by reminding Titus of the availability of divine resources (verse 4).

Warnings

Father-son talks aren't complete unless "Dad" warns "Junior" about bad company and bad habits. Timothy and Titus didn't miss out on this kind of advice, for Paul gave his sons in the faith good counsel about avoiding bad characters and bad practices.

In his first letter to Timothy Paul warned him to refuse religious fables (I Timothy 4:7). Such human inventions can't do anything but confuse people. Timothy was obliged as the minister of Jesus Christ to fill his thoughts and sermons with "the words of faith and of good doctrine" (verse 6).

Also, Paul warned Timothy not to let anyone despise his youth (I Timothy 4:12). The word "despise," which Paul used in his counsel to Timothy, carries the thought of pushing aside. Apparently, some bullies in the church were pushing Timothy around because of his young age for a pastor. So Paul was telling his "son in the faith" to stand up to those bullies and let them know by word and deed that he was God's man (verse 12).

Then, too, Paul warned Timothy to flee from the company of those who had nothing better to do than bicker among themselves over religious speculations and scheme ways to get rich at others' expense (I Timothy 6:5). Paul let Timothy know that covetousness is a poison that ruins a Christian's testimony in quick order (verses 9,10).

Finally, in his second letter to Timothy, Paul even mentioned the name of a person to avoid (II Timothy 4:14). It reminds us of a parent telling a son, "Stay away from that boy Billy down the street or you'll be sorry." It is a warning that springs from knowledge of human nature and carries an air of genuine concern.

Titus, too, received fatherly warnings from Paul. For example, in Titus 1:14 Paul told him what he had told Timothy—"Stay away from religious fables." Like Timothy, Titus was obliged as God's spokesman to speak "the things which become sound doctrine" (Titus 2:1). And Titus received the same kind of warning Paul had given Timothy about avoiding bickering over inconsequential religious matters (Titus 3:9).

Spending Time Together

Fathers often fall short of providing adequately for their children. Not in terms of failing to give them enough food, clothing, and things. In Western culture fathers usually go overboard in giving their children too much in these areas. The problem is they provide too little of what children need and want most—an available father. Spending time with a child is far more important than spending on a child.

As we have seen, Paul spent a great deal of time with Timothy and Titus during the formative years—those years following their conversion to Christ. He took them with him on his travels and gave them abundant opportunity to learn from him. During those years he poured his own personality and convictions into them.

Timothy and Titus must have treasured that period of life. What a privilege was theirs—the privilege of being so close to God's choice servant! But Paul must have treasured their company too, for later, when they were apart, he wrote to say that he wanted to see them again.

Paul was en route to Nicopolis to spend the winter when he wrote to Titus (Titus 3:12). It seems that he had been released from prison for a short time and was using that time profitably—making a fourth missionary journey. He was most anxious to be reunited with Titus during this time, so he requested Titus to "come unto me to Nicopolis" (verse 12). But at Nicopolis Roman soldiers seized Paul, arrested him, and returned him to Rome, where he spent the rest of his days on earth in a dank dungeon.

From that dismal Roman cell Paul's thoughts turned to Timothy. He wrote his second letter to Timothy—his last epistle of all the New Testament epistles that bear his authorship—and urged Timothy, "Do thy diligence to come before winter" (II Timothy 4:21a). The spiritual father longed to enjoy the company of his young son in the faith.

We Christians would do well to maintain the kind of relationship with our spiritual offspring that Paul maintained with his. Encouragement, warnings, and spending time with those whom we have won to Christ are important elements in directing them into a close walk with Jesus Christ. Let's be good "parents."

Chapter 11

Joy That
Just Won't Quit

What does it take to be happy? A pay raise? A vacation at Disney World? A new car? Perhaps a compliment from your better half? Most persons find happiness—at least for awhile—in favorable circumstances. But joy is something special. It doesn't depend on favorable circumstances. Nor is it short-lived.

Take Paul, for example. He had joy—the real thing—when circumstances were far from favorable. Interestingly, the letter to the Philippians, which has often been called "the Joy Epistle," was written by Paul when he was under arrest in Rome. He was in bonds, according to Philippians 1:7,13,14, but his spirit was not bound. It must have reached all the way to Heaven as he encouraged himself in the Lord.

Joy Overflowing

Read some of Paul's joy verses in Philippians and thrill to the reality of Christ in his life.

". . .making request with joy" (1:4)

". . .I therein do rejoice, yea, and will rejoice" (1:18).

"Fulfil ye my joy" (2:2).

"Yea, and if I be offered upon the sacrifice and service of your faith, I joy, and rejoice with you all" (2:17).

". . .my brethren dearly beloved and longed for, my joy and crown . . ." (4:1).

"but I rejoiced in the Lord greatly . . ." (4:10).

What about Today?

Does this kind of supernatural joy abound today among Christians? It ought to, for Paul commanded in Philippians 4:4, "Rejoice in the Lord alway." But does it?

In recent years Christian counseling has come to the fore as an essential part of the ministry. Today, any pastor with counseling skills and the good sense to know how to give Scriptural help for troubled hearts and homes doesn't have to hunt for work. His church members beat a path to his pastoral study. And depression is among the top problems they bring.

How do we account for this? Surely, if Paul

experienced joy in extremely adverse circumstances, shouldn't twentieth-century Christians in the lap of much more pleasant surroundings be able to have joy in their lives? Of course! But first there are conditions to be met.

"Rejoice in the Lord." Don't stop with the word "Rejoice" when you read Paul's command in Philippians 4:4. Read on. He wrote, "Rejoice in the Lord." Happiness depends upon favorable happenings, but joy depends upon a relationship with Jesus Christ that is conscious and consistent. As we focus our attention on Jesus Christ, we enter more fully into an appreciation of Him and what we have in Him. In turn, this well-founded appreciation sets the joy bells ringing.

What is involved in our relationship with Christ? Salvation, for one thing. The psalmist exulted, "My heart shall rejoice in thy salvation" (Psalm 13:5). Surely the assurance that God has acquitted us of all our transgressions and has freely bestowed sonship upon us gives us enough reason to rejoice. But there's more.

God takes good care of us. We may find ourselves locked in tough situations at times, but we are protected in all of them. God will not permit even the most severe trial to devastate us. His arms are around us to strengthen and comfort us. Isn't this what the psalmist meant by his testimonial, "But let all those that put their trust in thee rejoice: let them ever shout for joy, because thou defendest them" (Psalm 5:11a)?

The Scriptures are also a source of joy. As

we meditate upon them, recognizing that they have come to us from the Lord, we find numerous reasons to rejoice in the Lord. We find ourselves declaring, "Thy testimonies have I taken as an heritage for ever: for they are the rejoicing of my heart" (Psalm 119:111).

Our rejoicing in the Lord also involves the practice of simply adoring Him for who He is. When the disciples clustered around the risen Christ just before He ascended to Heaven, they basked in the glory of who He is. "They worshipped him, and returned to Jerusalem with great joy," according to Luke 24:52.

Undoubtedly Paul met the first condition for having joy. He rejoiced *in the Lord.* He appreciated what he had in Christ—salvation, an unfailing Defender, the heritage of the Scriptures, and Someone to worship who was victorious over death and the grave. What he had in *Christ* more than compensated for the troubles and pains he encountered *in the world.*

Rejoice *in the Lord*!

Serve the Lord. There's something therapeutic about serving Christ. When we are busily engaged in meeting others' needs, we are less likely to worry about our own needs. When we are actively ministering to others, we just don't feel any compulsion to drown ourselves in self-pity. Seeing God at work in the lives of those to whom we minister results in gladness and joy beyond compare. It is only when we divert our attention from the privilege of serving Christ to the cost factor—real or imagined—that we go searching for the crying towel.

The psalmist promised that those who sow in tears (not tears of depression but tears of concern) will greet the harvest with rejoicing (Psalm 126:5,6). Paul understood this. He welcomed every evidence of God's activity in the lives of others as an occasion to rejoice. He rejoiced when the Corinthian church displayed a spirit of hospitality (II Corinthians 7:13; 8:6). He rejoiced when an excommunicated member of the Corinthian church repented (II Corinthians 1:24; 2:3). He rejoiced when the believers in Macedonia gave generously to the relief of poor Jerusalem saints (II Corinthians 8:2). He rejoiced when the Thessalonians turned in faith to Jesus Christ (I Thessalonians 2:19, 20; 3:9).

Instead of wringing our hands over personal troubles we ought to stretch out our hands to lift the fallen. Instead of pacing the floor in endless worry we ought to walk in the paths of service. Instead of spilling out one tale of woe after another we ought to spell out the message of salvation and hope to others. Indeed the best way to improve our lot in life is to build a "service station" on it! Then we shall exclaim with joy, "I delight to do thy will, O my God" (Psalm 40:8a).

Obey God's Word. It is absolutely impossible to be a joyful Christian while violating God's written Word. Jesus promised His joy only to those who respond to His commands (John 15:10,11). As someone has observed, "Sin causes the cup of joy to spring a leak."

David found this out. His sin with Bathsheba robbed him of the joy he had experienced in walking close to God. He confessed his sin and pleaded with God, "Restore unto me the joy of thy salvation" (Psalm 51:12).

Fortunately, God does restore the joy of salvation to anyone who sincerely desires this restoration. A disobedient Christian can find the way back to the joy of the Lord. It is the way of confession of sin (I John 1:9) and obedience to the Scriptures. As he treasures and obeys the Word of God, he finds himself exclaiming, "The statutes of the Lord are right, rejoicing the heart" (Psalm 19:8a). And he becomes productive, like a tree planted by a waterway (Psalm 1:3). And you can count on it, this productivity will include joy along with the rest of the fruit the Holy Spirit develops in the life of every obedient Christian (Galatians 5:22).

This explains why Paul possessed uninterrupted joy, doesn't it? He obeyed the Lord consistently. He could say without the slightest trace of hypocrisy, "I was not disobedient unto the heavenly vision" (Acts 26:19).

Don't you agree that when we lose the blessing of joy we must face up to wrongdoing and renew our dedication to keeping God's commands?

Hope in the Lord. Sometimes—let's admit it—we Christians act like God isn't working on our behalf any longer. We suggest by our fretting and stewing that He has closed down shop and hung a "Business Closed Forever" sign on the door. There's really no excuse for this, for the Bible spills over with assurances that God never abandons us. It holds out to us the promise of hope—that God will perfect His will concerning us.

Paul's writings abound with such encouragement. He tells us that we ought to rejoice as we anticipate the fulfillment of His work in us. For example, here's what he wrote to the Christians at Rome: "By whom also we have access by faith into this grace wherein we stand, and rejoice in hope of the glory of God" (Romans 5:2); "Rejoicing in hope" (12:12); and "Now the God of hope fill you with all joy and peace in believing . . ." (15:13).

So let's not let circumstances get us down. Let's welcome circumstances as opportunities to look up and beyond—to the day when God's work in our lives will be complete and perfect. This will put joy deep within us and far out of the reach of even the most trying circumstances.

Chapter 12

Across
the Finish Line

The small-town high school had entered the track and field county-wide competition, and the coach was concerned. He had only one man on the team to enter in the two-mile event. He kept asking himself, "What am I going to do if something happens to my only two-miler?" He decided to share this concern with the whole team.

Gathering his track team around him, the coach explained, "Men, you know we have only one two-miler. Frankly, our showing at the county meet would be terrible if something prevented him from running. I think we need a back-up man—someone who can get into shape and be there when we need him for the two-mile race." Looking at Fred, the half-miler, the coach asked, "Fred, how about volunteering to be our man?"

Fred appeared startled. Then he lamented, "Coach, count me out. Any time I have to go that far I hitchhike."

Normally it's a long way from conversion to Christ to the end of the road. And, like Fred, some Christians prefer to hitchhike. This was not the case with the Apostle Paul. From start to finish he served Jesus Christ faithfully. Not even a dark dungeon in Rome, where he closed out his missionary career, dampened his enthusiasm for Christian service. Although he had a rendezvous with martyrdom, he knew that beyond the executioner stood Jesus Christ, waiting to receive him and present a victor's crown to him.

The Record of Faithful Service

From his dungeon cell Paul wrote his second letter to Timothy. As he closed the letter he testified triumphantly, "I have fought a good fight, I have finished my course, I have kept the faith" (II Timothy 4:7).

Paul used three metaphors to describe what his service for Christ had been like over the years. He compared himself to a wrestler, a runner, and a soldier.

Paul's word for "fight" points to the Greek wrestling matches in which men struggled against each other with all their might. It is a clear indication that the apostle regarded the Christian life as a struggle. And it surely is. We wrestle against demonic powers and our own sinful inclinations. The contest will not end until we are safe in the presence of our Lord. But neither Satan nor indwelling sin can pin us to the canvas as long as we draw our strength from our risen Lord. Paul's assurance throughout his wrestling match was, "I can do all things through Christ which strengtheneth me" (Philippians 4:13).

The word "course" in II Timothy 4:7 refers to a circuitous race, filled with obstacles. This suggests that Paul's run for God's glory was filled with difficulties. There were numerous hurdles to clear as Paul raced for the finish line. Again, Paul's testimony emphasizes that the Christian life is not simply a pleasant stroll through a rose garden with celestial music culling through the air to make the stroll even more pleasant. Quite to the contrary, the Christian life is demanding. It is filled with dangers. There are obstacles to surmount. But the toughness of the course makes winning all the more sweet.

Finally, Paul testified that he had kept the faith. The word "kept" carries the meaning of having guarded the faith as an armed soldier would guard his post against enemy attack. We know that Paul was indeed an able defender of the body of doctrine God gave to the church. He did not sleep at his post or let down his guard for a moment even when he was greatly outnumbered by the enemy. Now it remains for us to guard the faith.

Tough Discipline

A long time before Paul crossed the finish line to end a victorious race he had determined to discipline himself in order to be in top spiritual condition. He explained his philosophy to the Corinthians: "Know ye not that they which run in a race run all, but one receiveth the prize? So run, that ye may obtain. And every man that striveth for the mastery is temperate in all things. Now they do it to obtain a corruptible crown; but we an incorruptible. I therefore so run, not as uncertainly; so fight I, not as one that beateth the air: But I keep under my body, and bring it into subjection: lest by any means, when I have preached to others, I myself should be a castaway" (I Corinthians 9:24-27).

Anyone who has entered competitive athletics can appreciate Paul's philosophy. It takes hard work, vigorous training, and sacrifice to excel in athletic competition. Furthermore, an athlete must obey the rules or be disqualified.

In the 1976 Summer Olympics at Montreal more than a few gold-medal winners spoke of the strict discipline they adhered to in order to win. They trained for hours each day. They passed up parties and late nights in order to maintain their training schedule. They were loners for the most part, for they just didn't have enough time to socialize. And as they trained, and trained, and trained, they kept their eyes on the goal—a gold medal in Montreal. When they won the gold, it was worth all the effort and sacrifices.

Also in the 1976 Summer Olympics there was a disqualification. A member of the fencing team from the Soviet Union tried to bypass the rules to gain an easy victory. He knew that each time a competitor's sword touched an opponent it would trigger a light as a point scored. So he rigged his epee to light up whenever he chose—without touching his opponent. When the judges found out about his cheating, they put out *his light* and sent him home to Russia in disgrace.

Paul served Christ well. He was disciplined and carefully observed the rules. When he went home to be with the Lord, he did so as a victor.

Seizing the Crown

While Paul awaited the executioner, he thought about the greeting he would receive from the Lord when he entered Heaven. He thought about the crown that would be his. He wrote to Timothy, "Henceforth there is laid up for me a crown of righteousness, which the Lord, the righteous judge, shall give me at that day: and not to me only, but unto all them that love his appearing" (II Timothy 4:8).

What anticipation of a glorious entrance into Heaven! It can be compared in small measure to the thrill an athlete experiences when he stands in the winner's spot and receives the judge's congratulations and reward. He knows that every ache he encountered as he stretched every bit of muscle fiber to reach the finish line first was worth it.

It will be worth it all for us too if we run with patience the race that is set before us, as Hebrews 12:1 admonishes. It will be worth it all when we see Jesus and receive a crown of righteousness from Him. So let's welcome the discipline, pay the price that following Christ demands, and look forward to a glorious entrance into Heaven.

A number of years ago five young missionaries laid down their lives on the banks of a jungle river in Ecuador. The Indians they were trying to reach with the gospel had thrust them through with spears. It was a shock to the Christian world. But it was also a challenge and a lesson—a lesson to count no sacrifice too great in doing the will of God. Perhaps this lesson came home to hearts most emphatically through an entry one of the missionaires had made in his diary. It announced: "He is no fool who gives up what he cannot keep to gain what he cannot lose."

These martyred missionaries went home to Heaven in the best tradition. Like Paul, they had fought a good fight, they had finished their course, they had kept the faith. So let us take heart, and "press toward the mark for the prize of the high calling of God in Christ Jesus" (Philippians 3:14).

Just a few more days to be filled with praise,
And to tell the old, old story;
Then, when twilight falls, and my Saviour calls,

I shall go to Him in glory.

I'll exchange my cross for a starry crown,
Where the gates swing outward never;
At His feet I'll lay every burden down,
And with Jesus reign forever.